Dear Reader: Chris

The book you are about to read is the latest bestseller from the St. Martin's True Crime Library, the imprint *The New York Times* calls "the leader in true crime!" Each month, we offer you a fascinating account of the latest, most sensational crime that has captured the national attention. St. Martin's is the publisher of bestselling true crime author and crime journalist Kieran Crowley, who explores the dark, deadly links between a prominent Manhattan surgeon and the disappearance of his wife fifteen years earlier in THE SURGEON'S WIFE. Suzy Spencer's BREAKING POINT guides readers through the tortuous twists and turns in the case of Andrea Yates, the Houston mother who drowned her five young children in the family's bathtub. In Edgar Award-nominated DARK DREAMS, legendary FBI profiler Roy Hazelwood and bestselling crime author Stephen G. Michaud shine light on the inner workings of America's most violent and depraved murderers. In the book you now hold, WITHOUT MERCY, *New York Times* bestselling author and forensic psychiatrist Keith Ablow profiles a doctor who killed his own patients. What possessed him to do the unthinkable?

St. Martin's True Crime Library gives you the stories behind the headlines. Our authors take you right to the scene of the crime and into the minds of the most notorious murderers to show you what really makes them tick. St. Martin's True Crime Library paperbacks are better than the most terrifying thriller, because it's all true! The next time you want a crackling good read, make sure it's got the St. Martin's True Crime Library logo on the spine—you'll be up all night!

Charles E. Spicer, Jr.
Executive Editor, St. Martin's True Crime Library

# PRAISE FOR *WITHOUT MERCY*

"Dr. Ablow has produced a work that is interesting enough to be a page-turner."

—*Journal of the American Medical Association*

"Dr. Ablow not only provides detailed reconstruction of Kappler's troubled past, his crime and trial, but also a look at much broader, and just as terrifying, issues of competence in the medical profession."

—*North Shore Sun*

"The book poses the question put to the jury: Was this obviously mentally ill man capable of telling right from wrong?"

—*Boston Herald*

"An M.D. committing such depraved and violent murder. 'How can that be?' we ask. Dr. Ablow's superb investigative reporting goes as far toward answering that question while pointing out the danger of accepting pathological behavior in anyone, regardless of his degrees or stature in society."

—Michael S. Palmer, M.D.,
author of the *New York Times* bestseller *Natural Causes*

# PRAISE FOR THE AUTHOR

"I've thoroughly enjoyed and appreciated your *Washington Post* pieces. Aside from your obvious skill and sensitivity as a writer, you've honed in on topics that are of real concern to all of us."

—William Styron

## ST. MARTIN'S PAPERBACKS TITLES
## by KEITH ABLOW

*The Architect*

*Murder Suicide*

*Psychopath*

*Compulsion*

*Projection*

*Denial*

*Without Mercy* (nonfiction)

# WITHOUT MERCY

## The Shocking True Story of a Doctor Who Murdered

# KEITH ABLOW

Published in hardcover as
*The Strange Case of Dr. Kappler*

St. Martin's Paperbacks

The material in this book is drawn from interviews, published articles, court transcripts, and medical records. Many of the quotations attributed to individuals come from author interviews; others (including quotations from Dr. Kappler and his family) are taken from these other referenced sources.

Published in hardcover as *The Strange Case of Dr. Kappler*

Published by arrangement with The Free Press

WITHOUT MERCY: THE SHOCKING TRUE STORY OF A DOCTOR WHO MURDERED

Copyright © 1994 by Keith Russell Ablow.

Cover photograph courtesy Photodisc / Imagine.

Library of Congress Catalog Card Number: 94-19570

ISBN: 0-312-95736-X
EAN: 9780312-95736-0

Printed in the United States of America

The Free Press hardcover edition published in 1994
St. Martin's Paperbacks edition / July 1996
St. Martin's True Crime Library edition / August 2006

St. Martin's Paperbacks are published by St. Martin's Press, 175 Fifth Avenue, New York, NY 10010.

10 9 8 7 6 5 4 3 2 1

This book is for Dr. Paul Mendelsohn

Mender of wings,
restorer of flight,
may you wheel and soar
under the sun
forever.
—Harry Crews

# CONTENTS

And this again, that this insurgent horror was knit to him closer than a wife, closer than an eye; lay caged in his flesh, where he heard it mutter and felt it struggle to be born; and at every hour of weakness, and in the confidence of slumber, prevailed against him, and deposed him out of life.

—Robert Louis Stevenson
*The Strange Case of Dr. Jekyll and Mr. Hyde*

# PROLOGUE

Dᴇᴄᴇᴍʙᴇʀ 21, 1990

Dr. John Frederick Kappler, Jr., a wiry little man gone gray, stood next to his lawyer in the Superior Court of Cambridge, Massachusetts, to hear whether the twelve citizens charged to dispense justice had judged him an insane man or a cold-blooded murderer.

His wife and children, one of his daughters herself a lawyer, sat stiffly and silently at the back of the courtroom. So, too, did the family members of his victims.

It had been a little more than eight months that Kappler had been locked in psychiatric hospitals waiting for this day, watching the gears of psychiatry and the law grind their teeth on his mind, unsure whether in the end society would attempt to heal him or resolve to punish him. But this judgment on whether he should forever be thought evil or ill had been foreshadowed for decades.

He was, by any measure, a terribly angry man, and he may have been feeling some of the rage that had fueled his repeated acts of violence. He had never been able to tolerate the critical eyes of others, instinctively turning any anxiety or fear or embarrassment he felt into fury.

He looked for a moment at the prosecutor seated not

twenty feet away from him, who had asserted that he was a manipulative liar, repeatedly fabricating psychiatric symptoms to escape the consequences of his intentional destructiveness. In spite of the antipsychotic and mood-stabilizing medications he was taking, he may have been buoyed by voices reassuring him that he was extraordinary and untouchable by such a lesser being.

Perhaps there was sorrow in his heart for the pain his family had endured because of his destructiveness or a hint of remorse for what he had inflicted on his victims. Or perhaps he felt no more and no less than utterly alone, the only personal freedom he had ever achieved. He had remained silent throughout the trial, never taking the stand in his own defense. Whether found guilty or innocent, he could be confident that there was not a soul in the courtroom that winter day who would ever come close to knowing him.

# PART ONE

# FATAL CHAOS

# CHAPTER 1

Saturday, April 14, 1990, in Boston. The Charles River, just a few months ago another gray line in an urban winter, had reasserted itself in blue, drawing people to its edges and beyond. Sun off the mirrored Hancock Tower illuminated Back Bay buildings a century old. Green grass tenaciously recarpeted the Boston Common. Convertibles, sailboats, and tank tops appeared as acts of faith. It was the kind of awakening that can happen in a city that has survived an angry winter.

Just north of Boston in Medford, Dr. John F. Kappler, Jr., a sixty-year-old retired anesthesiologist and army veteran, sat down to a breakfast of croissants and coffee with family and friends. He and his wife, Tommie, a psychiatric nurse, had been visiting their daughter Elsie, a law student at Northeastern University. Her boyfriend, Stephen Bloom, was there. So was her roommate, Alex Pancic, and his girlfriend, Finula Roy.

John Kappler had left the couple's home in Van Nuys, California, on March 15, driving to Alabama, where Tommie had flown to meet him and visit with a mutual friend. Then the two had continued on together, stopping to see a relative in Florida, Tommie's brother in Georgia, and friends in South Carolina, North Carolina, and Virginia. They met their daughter Dana, son-in-law, and grandchild near Washington, D.C., and visited with their nineteen-year-old son, Jack, in New York City. After their arrival in Medford on April 11, they had explored Boston and visited the serene coastal towns of Gloucester and Rockport.

Now the visit with Elsie was over. Earlier that morning, after a night that included making love with her husband, Tommie had helped pack the couple's 1989 dark blue Hyundai Sonata for Kappler's drive back to California. He planned to stop again to visit with Jack, a student at New York University, and to spend Easter with Dana and her family. For reasons that remain unclear, Tommie had decided to fly home.

Kappler, a slight man at 5 feet 10 inches and 153 pounds, with sparse gray hair and green eyes, should have felt at one with a city resurrected. He had known despair. Several times over the previous three decades, he had been admitted to psychiatric hospitals, believing that people were after him or hearing voices commanding him to commit violent acts. Each time, medications seemingly brought him back to reality. And each time he had returned to the practice of medicine.

He had risen from the paranoia he reported in 1966 when he believed the CIA was stalking him, his house was bugged, and his wife was trying to poison him.

He had continued to practice medicine even after the chaos of 1975 when, by his own report, he heard voices demanding he give a pregnant patient the wrong anesthetic, risking her life. He signaled a cardiac arrest, though the patient had not suffered one. After calling cardiac arrests on two other patients that day, his colleagues in the operating room had told him to leave, and he had.

On the way home, he had crashed into another vehicle on the freeway, stolen that damaged car, and driven into another accident. He was jailed for several hours until his wife and a few hospital doctors picked him up.

Under the pseudonym Richard Q. Larson, Kappler had written an op-ed piece in 1978 for the *Los Angeles Times* about the emotional pain of that incident and how it allowed him to help a paranoid man he encountered on a bus years later. "Oh God, oh God, they're gonna get me," the man had said. Other passengers had laughed, and one had yelled at the man to stop ranting. But John Kappler had understood the man's terror:

I myself didn't laugh a bit: I remembered all too well how those who should have known better had laughed at me. On the occasion of my own breakdown, I'd been arrested after causing a public disturbance. Later, convinced that they'd kill me if I didn't please them, I sang both verses of "Danny Boy" to an assemblage of policemen and policewomen. They laughed, applauded and whistled as they might have for a free 10 minutes of Shecky Greene—a reaction that, to me, sounded straight from hell. They were even more amused when, having been put behind bars, I did a somewhat indecent Romeo and Juliet balcony dialogue, teaming up with a young male prisoner who was absolutely undone by it all and swore he'd hurt me if I didn't shut up. Inside, though psychotically forced to continue, I was dying with fear.

Kappler went on to suggest that self-hatred can fuel mental illness and violence:

But that's what it's all about. In most forms of insanity lie elements of self-loathing that can lead directly to self-punishment, self-destruction and, sometimes, to destruction of others. The internal miseries of insanity are almost beyond a sane man's understanding. We all hurt—Job really is man's most effective metaphor—but the curve of hurt is exponential in the insane. A long, hard look at the snake pit should be a must for all attendants who would beat up a patient for dirtying a bed or for all policemen who would shoot a crazy person merely for appearing to terrorize.

No, I didn't laugh at the crazy man on the bus. Instead, I eased up on him ever so gingerly. I didn't touch him. Speaking softly, I told him that he needed a friend. I told him that I was concerned for him, that I was afraid he'd be hurt or hurt somebody else. I told him that he needed a doctor, needed to be admitted to a hospital. I mentioned both County Hospital and Camarillo, but then, after giving him the dollar he'd asked for, I got off at my stop.

I pray to God that he found his.

Kappler had survived more of his own terror during 1980 when, by his report, the voices came back, demanding that he inject a potentially fatal dose of the local anesthetic Xylocaine directly into the bloodstream of a surgical patient. The patient suffered a cardiac arrest but lived. And John Kappler continued to practice medicine.

In 1985 he had been charged with attempted murder after being accused of unplugging a patient's respirator. According to his wife, a friend of theirs had called and asked Kappler to look in on the patient, a quadriplegic who had tried to kill himself. Tommie has said she told

Kappler's psychiatrist that voices had instructed her husband to turn the machine off, but with no one willing to testify to seeing him do it, the case was dismissed due to insufficient evidence.

This time Kappler was worried that his reputation had been so tainted by the charges and the accompanying media attention that he might be accused of any unexplained mishap occurring around him.

"If anything happens in a hospital and I don't have an alibi, I'm screwed," he told a newspaper reporter covering the case. He retired after another physician diagnosed him with depression, and he was deemed eligible for Social Security disability benefits. He kept his license to practice medicine, however, in California, North Carolina, and Georgia.

Having lived through such misery, John Kappler could have felt liberated in the unflagging love of his family and the allegiance of his friends. But even on this bright Saturday morning in New England, against the backdrop of a city renewed, he was again hearing the call to darkness.

Alex, Elsie Kappler's roommate, noticed that he seemed "edgy," "highly strung."

Tommie Kappler, who remembered her husband's past preoccupations with being poisoned, was concerned when he left most of his coffee and his croissant. He hadn't eaten much in Washington, either. In New York, her son had told her, John seemed "tired and slow." She had taken note during a tour of Boston two days before of how peculiar it was that he wanted so badly to give money to every homeless person he saw. She knew he had awakened at least once in the middle of the night while in Boston, commenting that he ought to take some of his lithium, a mood-stabilizing medication. But she didn't call a psychiatrist.

No one—not Alex, Finula, Stephen, Elsie, or Tommie—stopped John Kappler from getting in his car when he abruptly told the group that he had better get going. Antipsychotic and mood-stabilizing medicines were in the car with him—some of them self-prescribed—but he hadn't been taking any of them regularly and hadn't taken the antipsychotic for weeks.

Dr. Paul Mendelsohn, thirty-two, carrot-red hair caught by the wind, reached down to feet that seemed too big for him and pulled the laces tighter on his running shoes. He was on call for psychiatric emergencies and had phoned New England Medical Center to let the staff know he would be out for a jog. He checked to make sure his beeper was secure at his beltline and started out slow.

Six feet tall, with long arms and legs, he looked lanky at rest but surprisingly graceful in motion. Running transformed him, chasing away the traces of awkwardness and bringing determination into features that rested at kindness. Perhaps that was one reason it had become a serious pursuit. He was training for his fourth San Francisco Marathon.

Spring reminded Mendelsohn of his native Novato, California, and made him eager for the planned move back there just nine months away. Through three years of training in psychiatry neither he nor his wife Camille had embraced the East. They did not think it a gentle or tolerant place.

He quickened his pace and ran onto a footpath that paralleled the Alewife Brook Parkway in Cambridge.

The son of two pediatricians, Mendelsohn had come to Boston to learn his craft, bringing himself wholly to his work. His extensive knowledge of music seemed to translate naturally into an ability to appreciate the harmony and dissonance in his patients' words. In a quiet profession, his colleagues had learned that his reserve and lack of pretense belied great insight and a keen sense of humor. They thought him, already, a doctor's doctor.

The parallel between marathon and residency training could not have escaped him. The miles had made his thin torso muscular, defining it in places that had once been nondescript; the years on wards and in clinics had opened his eyes to the unconscious, training him to see unremitting patterns in the seemingly disconnected events that made up his patients' lives.

Neither gain had been easily won. Approaching the end of his training, he had not forgotten the sleepless nights in emergency rooms, the seemingly endless days on locked inpatient units. There had been physical and emotional walls that made him wonder at the insensitivities of a system entrusted to cultivate empathy.

It might have been the changes wrought in him by psychiatry training that had shaken his marriage. Camille felt Paul had become disconnected from his own feelings, and the couple had begun to talk of separating. Paul, in fact, had scheduled an appointment with a divorce attorney.

Was the impending loss of his marriage weighing him down that Saturday morning? Or was he able to take heart from the warmth of the sun, from the trees lining the path, their branches just hinting at new leaves? Maybe all the beginnings and endings faded from his mind for a moment as his stride lengthened, his arms and legs moving in perfect rhythm, his feet barely touching ground.

Kappler would later claim that he had been hearing voices even at his daughter's apartment, that by the time he started driving he felt "possessed." After days of quiet paranoia, the voices, by his report, were giving him specific instructions about where to go and what to do. "It was as if," he would later say, "...the car was being driven by someone else."

He drove down Winchester Street in Medford to Harvard Street, around a rotary at Powder House Road and around another rotary into light traffic on the Alewife Brook Parkway in Cambridge. He had traveled about two miles. According to witnesses and investigators, his expression was serious and intent, his hands tight around the wheel. He sped through a red light at about 10:35 A.M. before veering off the parkway at approximately thirty-five miles an hour. He jumped a six-inch curb, avoiding the trees lining the road, and then drove straight along the adjacent running path, without braking, aiming for Paul Mendelsohn. Kappler later recalled that a voice told him to "hit and run." "I felt like it was a duty to perform, and I performed it," he would later tell Frederick Kelso, a forensic psychologist appointed by the state to evaluate him. "I had no shame then, I have no shame now."

Mendelsohn turned to look over his shoulder, but could not escape. He was struck, hit the right side of the windshield, and was carried on the hood hundreds of feet before being thrown to the ground, already unconscious. A five-inch curved gash behind his ear was bleeding profusely. His skull was fractured.

Kappler then accelerated about one hundred yards along the path and hit his second victim, Deborah Brunet-Tuttle, a thirty-two-year-old mother and human services worker who was returning from the grocery store where she had bought, among other things, plastic Easter eggs for a hunt at her church. She, too, was carried and dragged. Several of her bones, including her pelvis, snapped.

Kappler later told Dr. Kelso, "When I first headed toward him [Mendelsohn], I was going to hit him on the center, and then I thought, no, I'd better hit him on the right.

"... If I'd have hit him on the left, he might have come through the windshield on my left, on my side.

"... I certainly wouldn't have been able to continue on for the second one.

"I felt I had to get, I was gonna get a second one. If I had been immobilized, I wouldn't have been able to proceed."

When later asked by another forensic psychologist, Ronald Ebert, what would have happened had no second victim been on the jogging path, Kappler responded, "I don't know what would have happened. I don't know. I don't know if I would have gone on looking for somebody else. She was so conveniently placed."

The voices, according to Kappler, told him to hide his car in a driveway down a nearby dirt road. He took about $300 out of the car, locked the doors, and walked by the scene of the accident, watching paramedics and police tending to his victims. He remembers thinking the sirens were a form of congratulations and that his family would be proud of him.

He walked a few blocks and hitched a ride with a motorist. He later told Dr. Kelso that he had asked her whether he could make a call from her home and was planning to strangle her there—to "commit mayhem," as he put it on another occasion—but she refused his request. He left the car without incident.

At 1:30 P.M. Tommie Kappler returned home from shopping and lunching with Elsie and found a message on the answering machine from her husband. "Oh," he said, "I thought I might catch you there. Maybe you could pick me up. I'll chat with you later."

"I guess I expected them to pick me up and congratulate me, say, 'A job well done,' " Kappler later told Dr. Ebert.

"There's something wrong," Tommie remembers telling her daughter. "Well, maybe there's been an accident. Let's call AAA."

She did not tell police officers about the message when they arrived at Elsie's home later that day. She did not tell them that her husband might be psychotic. And she initially gave an inaccurate description of what he was wearing. No one can know whether she was trying to afford him the chance to flee.

Kappler has said that he continued to wander for hours, still under the direction of voices that, he claims, literally told him whether to turn right or left, this way or that. Yet after inquiring of a local home owner as to the availability of real estate in the area, he coherently asked for directions and continued on to the Marriott hotel in Woburn, across from the Mishawum commuter rail.

At some point, he reportedly considered suicide. The voices, he later said, had instructed him to jump in front of a car on Interstate 95. He described the scene for Dr. Kelso: "I went up, and I very fearfully, perhaps I didn't reach a place quite, where I was going to attempt that, and then the voice said 'go over the fence,' and then I climbed over that fence. . . . I got up to where the cars were passing very quickly. . . . I think it was a matter of waiting for a car. . . . I had to find an interval between cars. . . . I couldn't . . . actually, the period of time was not very long before the voice let me off the hook."

Instead of killing himself, he rode the commuter rail to Boston's North Station and used the subway maps to get to South Station. He bought a doughnut and some milk and wandered around the Symphony Hall area. He later reported having the sense that Barbara Bush, the president's wife, might arrive by white limousine, that he would be involved in an attempt on her life, and then he would be shot by the police. But he had the presence of mind to travel back to South Station for the 12:15 A.M. Peter Pan bus to New York City and to stay on the bus while it made ten stops en route.

Mendelsohn and Brunet-Tuttle had been rushed to Massachusetts General Hospital. His life was slipping away; hers was less in danger.

The impact of the collision had jarred Mendelsohn's brain, causing extreme swelling. He arrived at the hospital unresponsive and began to have seizures minutes later. His white jogging suit was soaked with blood from the laceration on his head.

He had carried no identification on his run. None of the attending physicians or residents treating him knew who he was. But when his beeper sounded several hours later, one of them telephoned the New England Medical Center extension that appeared on the display. Dr. Jan Urkevic, the junior psychiatry resident covering the emergency room, answered and gave them Mendelsohn's name. To Mendelsohn, who had, no doubt, cursed waking to a beeper's shrill cry more than once, the staccato tones summoning him now would have seemed a bitter absurdity.

Over a dozen of the best doctors on staff—the director of the intensive care unit, general surgeons, neurosurgeons, and orthopedic surgeons—were called in to try to save his life. Together with nurses, they stood by his bed two and three at a time and manually pumped fluids into his body for hours. Two holes were drilled through his skull in an attempt to relieve the mounting pressure on his brain, now more than twice normal. Kidney transplantation was considered but thought futile. A pall descended on the intensive care unit as the clinicians realized they were losing one of their own.

By the time Camille Mendelsohn arrived, the combination of trauma and its treatment had left her husband's face unrecognizable. He looked barely human. Struggling with her own severely limited vision—Camille was legally blind—shaking, and in tears, she pulled back the sheet and identified him by the contour of his chest.

She was given his wedding band.

"I want you to know we did everything humanly possible," a doctor told her later. "He had the best care at arguably the best hospital in the world."

While John Kappler was still making his way to New York City, Paul Mendelsohn, never having regained consciousness, was placed on *Do Not Resuscitate* status. He was pronounced dead April 15, at 2:05 A.M.

Kappler arrived at the Port Authority in New York City, where it was raining, some time after 6:00 A.M. He had it in mind, he said later, that he might eventually go on to Mexico.

He checked into the Carter Hotel, a sixty-dollar-a-night fleabag at West Forty-third Street tucked between strip joints and X-rated movie theaters. His room was lighted by a single exposed bulb.

After sleeping for fifteen or twenty minutes on soiled linens, the voices, Kappler later reported, told him to start walking again. He bought a deli sandwich at a nearby restaurant and watched some porno flicks. For a dollar he could have stood in a darkened booth at a nearby peep show and watched naked girls bend over in an adjacent room. For three dollars one of the girls would have come closer and let him reach through a hole in the wall to spank her for 30 seconds.

Then he walked, for hours and hours, as far south as

Greenwich Village and as far north as Central Park. He wore holes in his light tennis shoes, and his feet blistered.

At about 4:00 P.M., the voices, by Kappler's report, suddenly left him. He felt panicked and desperately alone. "As long as the voice was with me...," he later told Dr. Kelso, "I felt secure. I didn't think the voice would let me down."

When the voices did abandon him, his concern was primarily for his family members, not for Mendelsohn or Brunet-Tuttle. He worried that Tommie and the others would be disgraced by what he had done.

"There was transitory guilt in New York City," he told Kelso, "when the voice left me, and I returned to sanity, and that cleared very quickly, well, not very quickly, over a period of days. It's going to be very difficult in the courtroom. They always desire remorse; it will be kind of hard to manufacture."

He went back to the hotel and called Tommie in Medford. "Tommie, I think I've killed two people," she remembers him telling her.

"Where are you?" Tommie asked. According to her, Kappler was crying too much to be understood clearly during parts of the call.

"There was an accident," she recalls saying, "and a man is seriously ill in the hospital, and another lady has been injured. The police think you were the one driving the car. They found the car and it's, you know, wrecked."

She told him the family already had consulted a lawyer—renowned criminal defense attorney Jonathan Shapiro, of Boston—and that he should stay where he was and wait for their son Jack.

She then called Jack and directed him to go to the hotel: "Your father is very upset and he's very confused. I think he's having a psychotic upset, and I think you'd better be very careful, and just go in and help get him to the Payne Whitney Clinic [a part of New York Hospital]."

She didn't call the New York City police.

Kappler, meanwhile, had thought again about suicide. He later reported having stuck his hand in some water and his thumb in an electrical outlet. Nothing much happened. He considered hanging himself, but worried about how he would look when Jack discovered his body and decided against it.

When Jack arrived at the Carter Hotel about a half-hour later, he couldn't find his father and called Tommie, who urged him to search around the hotel and at the Port Authority. (Perhaps she wondered whether Kappler was about to travel elsewhere.) Just minutes later, however, Kappler himself called Tommie from the hotel lobby. He seemed even more confused to her. "John, you've got to understand," she said, "you're sick. You've got to get to the hospital."

Jack called soon thereafter from the Port Authority, and Tommie arranged for him to meet his father either at the Payne Whitney Clinic or New York Hospital's emergency room.

Jack Kappler found him at the emergency room. "Walking in, I saw my father pacing . . . ," he would recall.

". . . He was really disheveled; he was very sweaty; and his hair was unkempt and hadn't been combed; and shoelaces were untied.

". . . He started to cry. And he said he was sorry for what had happened; and he was badgering on about that I wouldn't be able to finish my education and how horrible it was. I was trying to calm him down and telling him it would be okay and not to worry."

The Kapplers were ushered into a small room with two benches in it and two security guards posted outside the open door. As they waited, Jack later reported during his father's trial, "He said—he made a lot of vulgar references. . . . He talked about 'hosing.' He talked about 'eating pussy,' and me 'eating pussy.' " Jack later told Dr. Ebert that his father would "fall in and out of himself. He'd be dad and then all of a sudden he'd be this dirty, snively roach."

After John Kappler was interviewed by a doctor for twenty minutes, he asked the security guards whether they would get him and his son a couple of beers. Then, according to Jack's report to Dr. Ebert, his father's demeanor changed dramatically: "Sometimes he wouldn't move at all, other times he'd really shake. I saw him start to shake and shake. His legs were shaking more and more. He said son, son, and he leaped up and attacked me. We're about 4 to 5 feet apart. He gets up, stands up quickly and starts put-ting [*sic*] his hands around my neck. I had to really fight him off. I put a boot heel in the solar plexus and he kept coming! He came at me. I kept fighting the hands off and I got a good solid kick in the solar plexus, went back and then he started coming. His eyes! They were crazy eyes like a zombie, just pure drive. No soul! Just drive!"

The guards knocked Kappler down and pushed Jack out of the room. "I'm sorry, son, I'm sorry," Kappler yelled after him. "I tried to strangle him! Sorry, son!"

According to Kappler's report shortly after the incident, he believed that the people whose voices he had heard would be coming to take him and Jack away. By strangling his son, he hoped to save him from a worse fate than death. "The attempt [to strangle Jack] was half-hearted," he later told Dr. Kelso, "but I scared his behind off."

Kappler was admitted to a locked inpatient unit of the Payne Whitney Clinic.

# FIRST PERSON

While Paul Mendelsohn was struggling for his life, Kenneth Giuffre, an anesthesiology resident at Massachusetts General Hospital, called me at home. There was nothing unusual about the late hour. During medical school at Johns Hopkins, the two of us had sometimes talked on the telephone until early morning. I was fighting to keep my writing alive amid the demands of medical school rotations, and Ken was refining a real talent as a rock drummer. Even covering the wards together through the night, we found our conversations wandering outside the confines of academic medicine.

As natural allies, we had a private pact to help each other maintain equanimity in the face of seemingly unmanageable demands from our supervising residents. The basic tenet was Never Bleed. We had come to see surviving training as the equivalent of swimming with sharks; the instinctive feeding of the housestaff would only become more frenzied with evidence that injury had been inflicted. Whenever one of us noticed that the other was ready to react with anger, we would whisper those words.

"I'm on call," Ken said.

"How is it?" I asked.

"Busy." He paused. "Listen, I was wondering if you might be able to help us with a question over here."

"Sure."

"We have a doctor in the intensive care unit, unconscious, who was jogging and got hit by a car," he said.

"A doctor?"

"Actually, a resident . . . wearing a beeper from your psychiatry department. Any idea who would have been carrying that tonight?"

"I don't know. What does he look like?" I asked.

"Well, that's just it. You know how traumatic the intensive care treatment can be. Between the accident and the work we did, there's too much swelling." He paused, this time a little longer. "Someone said he might be from California."

"My friend Paul Mendelsohn is from California," I said. Even having spoken it, the link seemed unreal. Despite all the inexplicable deaths I have witnessed on medical wards, I irrationally assured myself that Paul's death was unlikely because he was too good to die.

I had also started bearing witness to the moment, and I sensed an absurd cliché in it, a twist of fate that read like a bad script. What resident hasn't joked uneasily about the horrible poetry it would be to die at the end of training—when, in our hearts, many of us feel we haven't begun to live.

Becoming a doctor is a fraternity of suspended animation. We defer our pleasures. From the moment we cut into our cadavers, we begin evolving away from the world around us and toward one another. We share terrors and exhilarations that do not translate well into words and therefore remain a private trust. Thirty-six-hour shifts test our faith. We see patients cured and see patients die. We make errors, sometimes fatal ones. We see the coexistence of precision and chaos in our work, and we come to believe that others could never abide the dichotomy. A mentor of mine once said, only half-jokingly, "Eventually, you find out there are really only two species on the planet: physicians and not-physicians."

We hesitate to judge one another. We know none of us is above reproach.

Years before, during our internship year, I had confided in Paul that I might have missed subtle signs of internal bleeding in an elderly woman critically ill with cancer. While I was on call overnight, she died in the intensive care unit. He heard me out and reassured me that I had done as much as anyone else could have.

On another occasion, while watching several doctors attempting to resuscitate a patient in the emergency room, Paul had commented that his workload would increase if the patient survived. "I've got too many patients on my service already," he had complained. Perhaps an outsider would have been taken aback, but I knew instantly that his words were innocent, the aftermath of too many nights without sleep.

John Kappler and Paul Mendelsohn both belonged to this exclusive medical fraternity, but where the threatened loss of one brought a small army of Boston's finest doctors to Paul's bedside, the psychiatric symptoms of John Kappler had led to a kind of back-alley treatment.

"We've heard it might be Paul," I remember Ken answering me. "Listen, why don't I meet you in the lobby? There are some other residents from your program here."

I hesitated. "Look, anyone from the program would know if it was Paul. He's tall with red hair."

"Keith, I don't think your friend's going to make it," he said quietly.

Later that night, I walked Camille Mendelsohn, whose

separation from her husband was now irrevocable, to his bedside.

"Well, then, that's it," she cried later. "That's just it."

Nearly a year passed after that night in the intensive care unit before I considered writing this book. Friends asked repeatedly whether I intended to put my thoughts to paper, but I worried that detailing Paul's death might minimize his life. Moreover, I felt guilty for not having taken the chance to know him even better than I did and wasn't sure I had a sufficient claim on his last moments.

I was also acutely aware of a fear of death in me that I have carried most of my life, probably the reason that I left the country shortly after Paul was killed and returned after his funeral. Writing this book would mean finally confronting not only his mortality but my own.

My reservations temporarily withstood an inexplicable connection between John Kappler and me. Just days after Paul died I received a call from David Feiven, a lifelong friend of mine from Marblehead, Massachusetts. Our families had lived next door to one another while we were growing up. His younger brother, Stephen, had gone on to attend New York University.

"You knew the psychiatry resident who was hit by a car, right?" he asked.

"He was a good friend of mine," I said.

"Strange," he said. "Stephen lives with the driver's son. Jack, I think his name is."

"Stephen lives with one of the Kapplers?" I asked.

"He's his roommate at NYU. Weird, isn't it?"

It *was* a peculiar coincidence, and for months it weighed on me. So, too, did my memory of how Paul had repeatedly urged me to devote myself more completely to writing.

Ultimately, I came to feel as if Kappler's story had

pursued me and that I was exerting a conscious effort to keep my distance from him. With that realization, I resolved to turn and look at the man who had run my friend down.

I sent Kappler a letter informing him of my decision to write about him and asking to meet. A brief reply from his lawyer, Jonathan Shapiro, stated that his client did not wish to be interviewed.

No one else in the Kappler family was willing to speak at any length either. "My father is in a great deal of pain," his daughter Dana told me. "It doesn't make him feel better to talk about these things. . . . It's not that I don't want to talk to you. I can't talk to you."

"The Kappler family will deal with this by itself," his daughter Elsie, who had by then graduated from law school, told me. "And each individual will deal with it privately, by himself or herself. You must understand, we are very private people."

Kappler's daughter Caroline refused to be interviewed. Tommie Kappler did not return my calls.

The silence of Kappler himself, the inaccessibility of the family he had fathered, and the sense I got from his daughters that one's pain isn't to be shared all hinted at the cauldron of unresolved emotions boiling inside him. As a psychiatrist, as a journalist, and as a friend of the man Kappler killed, I wanted to pierce it and let the truth out.

# PART TWO

# THE ROAD TO BOSTON

# CHAPTER 2

God damn the day I was born
and the night that forced me from the womb.
On that day—let there be darkness;
let it never have been created;
let it sink back into the void.
Let chaos overpower it;
let black clouds overwhelm it;
let the sun be plucked from its sky.
Let oblivion overshadow it;
let the other days disown it;
let the aeons swallow it up.

—*The Book of Job*, translated by Stephen Mitchell

Kappler was from Pittsburgh, but he had no plans to stop there on his 1990 cross-country drive. He had rarely returned, in fact, after his first year of college. He wanted to forget the place so much that he considered becoming a physician "an immediate cancellation" of his past. "I wanted status," he has said. "I knew that if I became a physician, the title doctor covered up a lot of deficiencies, and brought in a lot of income, too." Indeed, he had gone further than anyone from his home town would have expected. Hazelwood, his old neighborhood near the steel mills of South Pittsburgh, didn't produce many college graduates, let alone doctors.

John Kappler was born on October 10, 1929, to two tenth graders who had only married a few months prior to his birth. His being conceived out of wedlock was a kind of family secret and apparently a lifelong source of embarrassment to him.

His religious background was another source of stress. Kappler's mother, Martha Hoymeyer, was a Roman Catholic, his father, John Kappler, Sr., a Protestant. While the couple agreed to raise their son in his mother's faith, his father nevertheless made his distaste for Catholicism known.

Both parents drank and were violent toward each other and their son. There was nearly constant screaming in the house. Dishes were thrown. Fist fights broke out. The couple separated more than once.

"I saw him knock the hell out of my mother," Kappler has said. "He backhanded her, and she gave as good as she got. She was abusive, too."

"I can remember my mother physically attacking my father," he remarked on another occasion. "She was not a battered woman, by any means. It was more 60–40."

Kappler was beaten by both of them and he didn't fight back. His father's violence, he has said, was directed only at him and his mother, though, not his younger sister, Kay, or younger brother, Robert. He must have wondered why he and not his siblings was the target of his father's cruelty. How was he different?

Kappler learned early on that expressing his real emotions wouldn't get him what he needed. He would cry for long periods of time without being comforted. When he was six or seven years old, he remembers his father, a laborer in the steel mills and elsewhere, telling him, "I don't know how you can piss, John, if you cry so damn much."

At eight or nine years of age, while attending the Birmingham Elementary School, he learned more about the importance of keeping his real emotions in check as he stoically endured his father's brutal attempts to make a man of him: . . . "If my father caught me running from someone who I thought was going to harm me [a fellow playmate], he made me and the kid fight in the back yard. I was terrified at first [and then] with something resembling straight anger or rage, I would then pummel the hell out of the kid. . . . I've always dealt with problems that way. At first there is this feeling of terror. My solution is then to grab all the feelings of anger I can get to meet the challenge. It's not attractive in the social sense. . . . I've been a yeller and a screamer all my life. . . . I've regretted that approach. I've always wanted to be a more measured person, who wanted to be in control. On the other hand, I might have been a panty-waist if my father had not done that." Groups of neighborhood boys would watch the back-yard fights and yell, "Get mad, get mad." His mother apparently did nothing to stop it.

What was happening to Kappler at home was taking its toll at school. No one in his family had ever finished high school, and his parents weren't invested in his finishing either. And although Kappler's IQ has been tested in the above-average to superior range and his memory ranks in the very superior range, his grades in school were mediocre or worse. When he talked once of going to college, his father predicted he would fail at it, and his grandmother warned, "Don't aspire above your station."

At age twelve, after moving to a housing project and witnessing a particularly brutal family fight, he realized that he would have to break free of his environment or give up all hope for his future. It may have been then that his life turned into a quest to be rid not only of his real and troubling emotions but of his roots. He already had more than his share of experience redirecting the sadness and fear of those years into resolve.

He may have sensed a first chance at recreating himself when he was placed outside his neighborhood for high school, in the Taylor Allderdice class of 1947. The school was in an upper-middle-class, Jewish area and prepared students for college. Its motto: *Know, Do, Be.*

Allderdice may have hinted at freedom for Kappler; but it must also have been painful for him. He was ashamed of his humble origins, something he couldn't conceal from the student body, a privileged group that wasn't always forgiving of diversity. John Orris, a friend of Kappler at the time and fellow choir member, remembers the two of them being among the poor students in the upwardly mobile community. "We were dragged along in it," he said. "We dressed more shabbily. . . . We had to have a lot of moxie to survive that." Another choir member, Shelly Morov, remembers the many fraternities and sororities at the school contributing to "a snobbish attitude."

The choir director tried to help Kappler and Orris. Emma Steiner was revered in the school for her dedication and her insistence on excellence. "We were in an elitist group, the a cappella choir," Orris said. "She told us how good we were and how we'd better prove it to everyone. It was like a Marine syndrome." But if Kappler considered himself a member of an elite group at Taylor Allderdice, his yearbook inscription to Orris—"Remember the craphouse quartet"—didn't show it.

Orris recalls Kappler being outspoken. His forthrightness, however, seems to have been reserved for students from backgrounds similar to his own.

Another friend of Kappler, Eunice Dobkin, remembers him as "a little thin kid with steel-rim glasses, very shy and to himself." She had the sense—correctly, it turns out—that he was working below his potential. "Something," she said, "seemed to be wasting his intelligence."

"I always wondered the kind of background he came from," Dobkin said. "A lot of people from Allderdice were clotheshorses and dressed, and John never did. I always thought, 'Maybe he's poor, or maybe something's wrong at home. . . . ' I think in high school I was one of the few people John warmed up to. I'm a physician's daughter and a child of divorce. Maybe he could sense that. I do feel he was an extremely sensitive person.''

Many of the most popular and active members of the class don't remember Kappler at all. Grace Harris, the editor of the 1947 yearbook, couldn't place him. ''I am very, very confused,'' she confessed. ''I have no idea who he is, and that's peculiar because I was the only editor of both the January and June classes [numbering 500, collectively]. I thought I knew *everybody*. . . . He must have been very quiet.'' Harris confirmed the split at Allderdice between haves and have-nots.

''It was very important at Allderdice where you came from. It was divided,'' she said.

Donald Sherrill, a popular cheerleader and homeroom president, was also confused. ''I knew everybody, but that name doesn't ring a bell,'' he said.

Charles Solof, a member of the student council and the social committee, commented, ''I don't know him at all. I would have sworn I'd never heard of him.''

Marcia Rosenheck recalls being in chorus with Kappler but admitted, ''I did not know him or anything about him.''

Stanley Simons, the tenth-grade treasurer and another student council member, remembered him vaguely as ''sort of a nonperson.''

Maurice ''Sonny'' Rosenblum, the class president in tenth and eleventh grades and one of the school's most active students, was shocked to ''have no memory of him.''

Lois Weiss, a majorette and charm club member, had ''no recollection'' of Kappler and concluded that he "must have kept a very low profile."

"He stayed out of sight," according to Maurice Amdur, a member of the student council, social committee, and orchestra.

The thirtieth reunion committee couldn't find Kappler, finally listing him as "unlocated" in its 1987 publication.

If Kappler felt different from and shied away from those of means, he also felt that his intellect and his drive separated him from the boys in his neighborhood, something he sensed they understood. His plans for his life ranged so far beyond theirs that they could have contributed to his living in a kind of no-man's-land: Alone at home. Alone at school. Alone on the street corner.

When Kappler turned fifteen, the few traces of stability in his life began to vanish. In that one year, his brother, Robert, died of a form of cancer called lymphosarcoma; his mother gave birth to twin girls, Annie and Edna; and Kappler's father left home for good.

When he lost his brother, Kappler apparently suppressed his grief, as had become his habit. "I had a brother," he would comment many years later, "who really is just a comma in my history." One family member, in fact, remembers him stating that he was glad Robert had died.

Some of Kappler's despair seems to have begun to leak out, however—as lawlessness. He stole a car, rode it around town with a friend, and then, he said, "wrecked it into a funeral home." He spent three days in juvenile hall. There were other more minor brushes with the law as well.

He chose to live with his father—perhaps the lesser of two evils in his mind—but felt increasingly responsible for his mother and sisters, who had little, if any, financial support.

To avoid being trapped in a dead-end job, he again turned worry over his future into the fuel for an extraordinary degree of determination. He applied to the University of Pittsburgh and was conditionally accepted. While living in a rooming house with his father and working a job to help support the family, he received all A's as a prelaw student his freshman year. Yet despite his academic success, he must have felt socially isolated. How many of his classmates could have imagined that he worked a second-shift job and then went "home" to study in a boarding house?

His family was proving to be more of a financial burden than he could shoulder. With his money running out, he could feel circumstances conspiring to rob him of his potential—to chain him to Pittsburgh forever, to make of him a laborer, like his father. He quit school and joined the army on the GI bill, resolute that he would never return to his birthplace once he was gone.

In preparation for his departure he went to see his mother. Whatever brand of abuse she had meted out over the years had left him in a quandary: He felt extremely angry at her, yet paradoxically responsible for her and dependent on her for approval. He asked her to list her debts and then spent whatever money he had left trying to retire them. "I wanted to clear her name," he has explained, "and clear me because I was leaving."

On entering the army, Kappler trained as a teletype operator in Kentucky and then shipped out to Korea on combat status for several months. While there, he ran a radio relay station and went from the rank of private to that of sergeant first class, earning a meritorious bronze star. He was usually far away from the enemy, seeing close combat only for a matter of days.

Military training may have added to Kappler's propensity to deny his weaknesses and fears, to safeguard against any chance of his becoming, in his words, a "pantywaist." He has said that his time in the service helped him by giving him an education in "living with men."

He wasn't always successful in maintaining a military bearing, however. Once when he had been drinking, he apparently became unruly and was picked up by the police. On another occasion, after many hours of exhausting work, he had gone to bed, only to be awakened by a superior officer. He wanted to get back to sleep.

"The army requires you to follow my orders," the officer had said.

"Oh, fuck the army," Kappler replied.

Kappler has said that the incident resulted in a summary court-martial, at which he was acquitted.

His fantasy of leaving behind what he has called the "quagmire" in Pittsburgh was proving futile. He continued to feel responsible for his mother and the twins and would send them part of his pay.

What sort of a man had John Kappler become?

He had had the misfortune to be a physically slight boy growing up in a violent, alcoholic home, in a neighborhood where he had been targeted for harassment.

His father, a man's man who didn't abide signs of weakness, had turned him over to bullies when he would run from them.

His mother was a manipulative and unreliable woman whose warmth could change unpredictably to hostility. When she had hit him, he hadn't defended himself.

His sister Kay, with whom he was particularly close, had been abused by their mother without him being able to protect her.

He had watched his brother, Robert, die a painful death from cancer without being able to save him.

He had quietly endured being visibly poor in a school filled with affluent students.

He may never have felt safe.

He had learned to keep his emotions, especially his terror, a secret. When he needed to, he had developed the ability to summon enough pent-up hostility to obscure any feelings of grief or fear.

He had already used a car as an instrument of destruction. "I've always associated his anger with cars," a family member who wished to remain anonymous said. "I remember him getting rageful in cars."

He had considered using his quick mind to arm himself with the power inherent in being a lawyer. When that seemed impossible, he had armed himself by joining the army.

He had created some distance between his core self and the self he showed the world. He may have felt so vulnerable inside that he couldn't—or believed that he couldn't—risk letting anyone know.

# CHAPTER 3

Kappler met his wife at a USO dance after he had returned from his service in Korea and was stationed at Fort Stewart in Hinesville, Georgia. Tommie, a plain, refined woman who was taller than Kappler, had recently completed her bachelor's degree and was working as a psychiatric nurse. She came from an educated Episcopalian family in Georgia that enjoyed status and had money. Her father, a full colonel in the military, and her brother were dentists. Like Kappler, she had been touched by tragedy. Her younger brother Dan had died in a fire while she was babysitting him.

Falling in love with this woman outside his social class and religion seems to have left Kappler in a terrible predicament: a point of departure from the life he had longed to be rid of was at hand, but the exit seemed blocked by his conflicting feelings of bitterness and obligation toward his family back in Pittsburgh. His mother had fallen ill with cancer, and the twins were still young and in need. What a futile gesture it must have seemed to him now that he had paid off a few of his mother's bills before leaving for the army. He must have thought then that his account with her was balanced. It was apparent that it was not. He grew deeply depressed and told Tommie that he wanted to break off the relationship.

Biologically minded psychiatrists have advanced a theory that depression is the result of imbalances of chemical messengers, called neurotransmitters, in the brain. Nevertheless, many psychiatrists continue to understand depression as a sign that the mind's psychological defense mechanisms—those mental gymnastics by which we keep unbearable memories out of consciousness—are feeling the strain of undeniable realities and are at risk of being overcome by them. In other words, the unthinkable is trying to force its way into one's thoughts.

Kappler may have tried to keep reality at bay by drinking, like his father and mother. Although it is not clear that he was ever addicted, he had enough reason to vow more than once during his life to never touch alcohol again.

He could have taken his depression as a warning that he was paying a price for keeping the real and injured parts of himself under wraps, but he apparently couldn't bring himself to share them. He went to a psychiatrist on the military base, but kept his distance from him. "I'll tell you exactly what happened," he told Dr. Kelso. "I didn't really talk to him.

"When I met my wife, I liked her very much, and she thought I was a pretty fair fellow. Sometime after we started dating, I got into a terrible blue funk. . . . I was going up to Fort Knox, Kentucky, for a mine and booby-trap school and I read an article on melancholia [an older term for major depression], and I realized that's what I had. I went to the psychiatrist on the post. His disinterest just came through, and I figured I'd work this out by myself."

Perhaps Kappler was right that the psychiatrist was indifferent to his problems. It's also possible that he thought

Kappler's symptoms were simply the result of recent stress or the manifestation of a chemical imbalance. Biological theories about the causes of mental illness were brand new then, and many psychiatrists were captivated by them. But even if the psychiatrist had been inclined to connect empathically with Kappler, he would have had to work diligently to overcome his patient's defenses against intimacy. Perhaps he failed to put forth the effort. For someone like Kappler traveling through life incognito yet longing for true understanding, anyone who takes the disguise at face value may be regarded as uncaring, unskilled, or simply a fool.

Working out his depression by himself meant meeting with his mother, then sick with cancer, to lobby for his freedom. He has said that he had become determined to marry: "My mother had suggested when I grew up I would take care of her. So, when I fell in love with my wife . . . I immediately became guilty. . . . I had to visit my mother, and just had to talk it out. I somehow came to an understanding [with my mother] that she would let me off the hook. I was truly the chattel of an Irish Catholic mother."

The extent of the anger Kappler felt toward his mother became clear many years later when his father asked him to prevent her from suing him for additional money. "Suddenly I had a weapon to bludgeon my mother," he told Dr. Ebert. He called and warned that he would embarrass her in court by revealing that his father had married her only because she was pregnant, to give her a "good name." She backed down.

Kappler's depression resolved in about three months, and the couple married in 1953. "Without any question," Kappler has said, "the most significant event in my life, one that I've become capable of experiencing in a dispassionate way, was my marriage. I was married, am married, to a woman much brighter than I, who managed to make me feel that I was the brighter one. I might say, not only her, but her family. My own family, I was estranged from.'' He further distanced himself from his past by converting to Tommie's religion and returning to college at Emory University in Atlanta, where her father and brother had been educated.

But tragedy seemed to be stalking them. His and Tommie's first child, a daughter named after her, was born with a cancerous tumor called a neuroblastoma above her left kidney. The primary growth was removed, but metastatic lesions were found, and the child required radiation treatments.

Kappler persevered in his studies. He had planned to become a dentist, like his father-in-law, but when a friend he admired became a physician, Kappler realized that his own grades were good enough to bring him a similar level of prestige. He applied to and was accepted by the Bowman Gray School of Medicine in North Carolina.

By then, Kappler had erased the visible traces of the poverty and abuse of his childhood, but he had not truly healed the internal wounds.

What sort of relationship had John Kappler escaped his mother for?

''His southern accent was like Tommie's southern accent,'' Frank Miller, a psychiatrist who was a medical school classmate of Kappler, recalls. ''He did everything to be like his wife and her family. He even converted to her religion.''

''I always thought it [the southern accent] was put on,'' Jack Kehoe, another psychiatrist who had been a medical school classmate of Kappler, said. ''I do recall the two of them being together in a way I had never experienced before. . . . I think Tommie was more controlling than healing. She had great rectitude and formality and direct-ness."

"She really kind of mothered him," Dotty Kehoe, Jack's wife at the time, remembers. "Whenever he would say something weird, she would say, 'Now, John.'"

There are fine lines between comforting a man, moth-ering him, and controlling him. Perhaps the distinction in Tommie's case was unclear to Kappler himself. He seemed to have difficulty determining her intentions to-ward him. Several times during their marriage he won-dered whether she was trying to kill him. And at least once, according to Kappler, he "might" have thought of killing her.

A source close to the Kappler family remembers two episodes, in fact, when Kappler became so enraged with his wife that he grabbed her by the neck and had to be pulled away from her. "He was a wimp manipulated to the extent that he had no control over his home or his wife," this person, speaking on condition of anonymity, said. "Maybe he was tired of it."

Bowman Gray classmate Robert Jones, who went on to become a pathologist and to settle in Birmingham, Ala-bama, considers himself Kappler's best friend from med-ical school. "John and I are very close friends and have been for years," he told me. "Nobody's kept in contact with John except me." Like others in Kappler's inner circle, however, he refused to reveal what he knew about him. And it remains unclear how close Kappler got to anyone during medical school.

Kappler had chosen Bowman Gray because it was small and seemed socially and academically manageable. But he still felt out of place. Alone, again.

"I never felt secure, regardless of my grades," he told Dr. Ebert. "I always felt insecure. My background was very different from that of everybody else, all middle class and upper middle class.''

Several classmates remember him as serious and very intelligent.

Mary Ward, now a pediatrician living in Georgia, described him as ''an extremely intense and inquisitive person'' who was ''very serious about his medical education.'' His intellectual capacity ''was extraordinary.''

No one seemed to know much about his background.

''He never said he was from Pittsburgh,'' Frank Miller recalls.

''I spent a ton of time with this guy and developed great attachment to him, but I didn't know him,'' Jack Kehoe said. ''. . . I know nothing about where he's from or anything else.''

What these two men did know was that Kappler, usually formal and professional, could become enraged unpredictably. His unwieldy stores of anger made them uncomfortable.

Kehoe accidently opened an innocuous-looking piece of mail addressed to Kappler. ''He just *blew* up,'' Kehoe remembers. ''I remember his energy and his anger and his clarifying his boundaries in no uncertain terms. I incorrectly assumed that I had a little leeway with him.''

Miller faced the same fury when Kappler heard rumors of his womanizing. ''He gathered I was doing this, that, and the other thing with women and he was very angry. I thought his eyes would come out of their sockets. . . . He was huffing and puffing.'' While Kappler was quick to label Miller's behavior as immoral, he himself watched pornographic films, has said that he indulged in ''unusual'' sexual practices, and has reported having had at least one affair during his marriage.

The secrecy surrounding his early life experiences, the

rigidity of his personal boundaries, and the energy with which he spoke out against feelings he might have harbored himself attest to Kappler's need to keep others from gaining insight into him. He had refined a persona that could work like a shield. To be known was to be vulnerable.

He tried to keep his daughter's illness a secret, as well. She died when she was three years old, during her father's second year at Bowman Gray.

"That was a very hard time," Kappler has said. "We toughed it out ourselves, nobody in our class even knew our child was dying."

Dotty Kehoe sensed Kappler was hiding his true thoughts behind a smokescreen of provocative statements: "He would always take unpopular stands—bizarre, weird stands—and defend them against all odds. But I couldn't tell if he really meant it."

Even Dr. Jones, after hearing about Kappler's life in Pittsburgh, seemed to abandon his conviction that he knew him so well. "My wife thinks he's crazy, anyway," he said. "She thinks he ought to be locked up. . . . Maybe the son-of-a-bitch is crazy."

# CHAPTER 4

These people must not learn who I am.

—Adolf Hitler, 1930

John Kappler graduated from medical school in 1960. He served as an intern in Charleston, South Carolina, lived for a time in Lenoir, North Carolina, and then finally decided to buy a general medical office being sold by a physician in California. He, Tommie, and their new daughter, Dana, moved to the West Coast, but the doctor reportedly decided against selling his practice, and Kappler had to build his own.

Why did the doctor back out of the deal? Did he not want to leave his patients, or did he sense something about John Kappler that made him uncomfortable putting their lives in his hands?

As it turned out, Kappler didn't like general practice at all—not the unpredictable calls, not the uncontrollable emergencies, and especially not the ever-present threat of becoming connected with people. Being a general practitioner means being part of the lives of many families over the course of many years. It means being accessible—touching patients emotionally and physically. It is not safe ground for those with inviolable personal boundaries.

"I didn't have the heart for general practice," Kappler has said.

Kappler's medical school classmate Frank Miller

agrees: "I don't think he'd be able to take general practice. Psychologically, he would find it impossible."

The stress of practicing general medicine may have brought Kappler's rage even closer to the surface. "He was different, all right," Dr. Robert Egan, Kappler's physician at the time, recalls. "He would just fly off the handle. John's responses were exaggerated . . . bizarre . . . overreactive for a given circumstance. . . . He was a very angry man."

Dr. David Barnes, Kappler's friend and his dentist, sensed the same instability. "You could say at that time he might become violent . . . ," he said. "He was much more volatile and emotional than people you'd usually see."

The family was growing. Kathryn Page Kappler was born in 1961, Elsie Bennett Kappler in 1962, and Caroline McNairy Kappler in 1963. But there was also more grief for the couple to bear amid the joys and stresses of a new home, four young children, and a new business. Tommie's father died in 1963 and her mother in 1964.

A year later, having already lost a brother, a daughter, and a father-in-law he loved, John Kappler lost more ground in the race he was running against his inner self. He began to feel terribly depressed, as he had in the army, and physical symptoms—excruciating chest pains—visited him as well. He was admitted to the intensive care unit of Hoag Hospital in Newport Beach. Some of the clinicians treating him there felt his chest pain might be psychosomatic—related to his underlying anxiety and hostility. A medical workup in the intensive care unit, in fact, revealed no clear cardiac problem.

The inability or refusal to acknowledge emotional suffering, whether in oneself or in others, has long been considered a growing place for psychosomatic illness. Anger, shame, and frustration that go unexamined and undiffused become caustic, as if they would eat their way out of the body.

Kappler himself has been diagnosed with stomach ulcers, a hiatal hernia and erosive esophagitis, a severe inflammatory condition affecting the esophagus.

Kappler's doctor, according to Tommie, told him that he would never be able to return to the profession, and he sold his practice. Despite this second episode of depression, Kappler still didn't dedicate himself to ongoing psychotherapy. Even after killing Paul Mendelsohn decades later, in fact, he seemed to have no interest in examining his life, or no capacity to do so.

"... I had various nervous breakdowns, to be euphemistic," he told Dr. Kelso, "and each of these changed me a little bit. But I found when each of these breakdowns cleared, I was happy to forget it, right up until the most recent, which I hope and believe will be the last. . . ."

The loss of his professional identity must have been devastating for Kappler. He had relied on it to conceal his deficiencies, to cancel his past, to win respect. Without it, he must have felt penetrable. The armor of his false self, built up so painstakingly for so many years was rusting away, revealing the weak, submissive, frightened, impoverished John Kappler no one—not even Kappler himself—was ever supposed to see.

He went to see a psychiatrist named Ronald Monaco in Newport Beach. The depression resolved somewhat over the course of several weeks or months, yet he seemed to be sealing himself over rather than opening himself up. "He used a lot of denial," Dr. Monaco recalled. "He had very little insight. This wasn't a man who was looking at himself in any great depth."

Then Kappler seems to have instinctively—and quite literally—sought cover again. He responded to an advertisement recruiting physicians for work with the Central Intelligence Agency. Some correspondence between him and the agency apparently followed. But before long, his fear of exposure seems to have ripened to psychotic proportions. He began to believe that he was being followed by the CIA, that his home was bugged, and that family members had been recruited to monitor him. He was confused and unsure what was real and what wasn't. He seemed to be lost in the very hall of mirrors he had built to escape others.

"The individual's apparently normal and successful adjustment and adaptation to ordinary living is coming to be conceived by his 'true' self as a more and more shameful and/or ridiculous pretense," psychiatrist R.D. Laing wrote on the evolution of psychosis. ". . . His 'self,' in its own phantasied relationships, has become more and more volatized, free from the contingencies and necessities that encumber it as an object among others in the world, where he knows he would be committed to be of this time and this place, subject to life and death, and embedded in this flesh and these bones. If the 'self' thus volatized in phantasy now conceives the desire to escape from its shut-upness, to end the pretense, to be honest, to reveal and declare and let itself be known without equivocation, one may be witness to the onset of an acute psychosis.

"Such a person though sane outside has been becoming progressively insane inside. Cases of this kind may present on superficial examination a most baffling problem since, on reviewing the 'objective' history, one may find no understandable precipitating stresses or, even in retrospect, any obvious indications that such a sudden abrupt form of events was imminent."

With Dr. Monaco's help, Tommie had her husband admitted to St. Joseph's Hospital in Orange, California, then known as the Benjamin Rush Neuropsychiatric Center, in June 1966. While there, he complained that the watch he had been wearing might have caused his chest pains and that pictures on the walls were agents of enemy forces. According to Tommie, Kappler later told her he had been hearing voices. He was diagnosed with schizophrenic reaction, paranoid type and treated with antipsychotic medication.

The diagnosis of schizophrenia, however, may have obscured even more ominous mental processes underlying Kappler's symptoms.

According to compelling psychological theories, schizophrenics withdraw from the world in order to insulate their core beings from what they perceive as deceit and chaos around them. Their symptoms, usually chronic and apparent to others, develop in this private, and ultimately suffocating, realm. Unable to form intimate or even social bonds with others, they generally cannot sustain marriages or highly skilled employment.

Other people who are faced with similar untenable emotional demands react quite differently. They turn outward, not inward, disavowing their core feelings, rejecting the idea that they are in pain and seeking a powerful position in an effort to stave off their feelings of inadequacy and self-betrayal. Such people, commonly known as psychopaths, become experts at blending with their surroundings and seem to interact with others relatively normally on the surface. But underneath their apparently successful relationships or careers lurk primitive rage and vengefulness.

Both schizophrenics and psychopaths (now commonly referred to as having antisocial personality disorder) can lose touch with reality—becoming paranoid, hearing voices or seeing visions—but the causes and psychological mechanisms underlying the disintegration may be different, as psychoanalyst Arno Gruen has noted. Schizophrenics, he says, "struggle from earliest childhood against surrendering to a reality that mocks their longing for genuine love." Psychopaths "attempt to conform to social reality at the cost of their inner truth. They collapse when outer reality no longer sustains them because its contradictions have become too obvious and crass." In other words, psychopaths suddenly "break down" when they are threatened with failure or loss of esteem, which terrifies them by hinting at how fragmented they really are inside.

After about six weeks on medicine in the hospital, Kappler's mental status cleared, and he was discharged. But was Kappler really healed or had he, with the help of medication, managed to camouflage his suffering, again? He was still the same man, after all, with the same life story and the same vulnerabilities. Had he purged himself of his demons or merely quieted them?

Within two weeks, he found work with Allergan Pharmaceuticals in Irvine, California, helping to promote new medicines. The job, however, offered little of the professional distance and narcissistic gratification he had counted on. As a practicing physician he had become infuriated when nurses, who took the liberty routinely with other doctors, failed to acknowledge his title and called him by his first name. Now people regularly used his first name. Tommie remembers his being bothered by having to "take orders from salesmen." His position didn't provide him with enough power.

On business in Chicago, he lost control. He stopped making sense and began to wander the streets throughout the night. He reportedly believed he had been drugged and that he was being followed. His alarmed co-workers suggested he call Tommie, who spoke with him and arranged for him to fly home. When she and a friend met him at the airport, he was disheveled and confused.

In the car on the way home, he appeared distracted. "He seemed to be—he wasn't addressing the conversations just to us," Tommie has said. "He seemed to be listening to—as if there was somebody else in the car with us. And I had a hard time communicating with him, and I'd say, 'Are you—what's wrong? Do you hear something or what's the matter?' And then he'd just look at me with a real weird smile and sort of glassy-eyed."

Kappler was admitted to St. Joseph's Hospital for another six weeks. According to the doctor treating him, he was depressed and paranoid. He spoke of the CIA's stalking him, wondered whether the candy Tommie had brought him might be poisoned, and complained of chest pain that again seemed to be a by-product of his psychological state. And again he was diagnosed with a paranoid schizophrenic reaction.

"He was confused," Tommie has said. "He was—he seemed to sit and not say much when I was there. He seemed hostile towards me. He seemed suspicious of me, of—when I would talk about anything, he seemed suspicious and asked me questions about everything that I said, you know, even if I was talking about children or whatever, he would question me very carefully, as if I wasn't telling him the truth."

When Tommie brought him a yellow shirt, he refused to wear it, thinking it symbolized his cowardice.

Treatment with tranquilizing and antipsychotic medications improved his symptoms, and he was discharged to home in September 1966. Tommie thought he still seemed ill. She told Dr. Kelso that her husband "had these bizarre requests—he wanted to go to this motel."

Despite his obviously fragile mental status, despite his having been hospitalized for psychosis twice within three months, despite his having felt stressed by seeing patients, John Kappler and his wife decided within weeks that it was time he went back to the practice of medicine. He applied to the University of Southern California for a residency in anesthesiology and was accepted.

Training began in October, not two months after leaving the psychiatric ward. He stopped taking antipsychotic medication and then stopped seeing Dr. Monaco. As he has said, he was happy enough to forget the chaos that had visited him.

What was really wrong with John Kappler? Was his bizarre thinking and behavior due in large part to the untenable separation of his true and false selves, to a dread of exposure ripened to malignant paranoia? Or were his "breakdowns" purely the result of a chemical imbalance in his brain?

Researchers have long known that the activity of a brain chemical messenger called dopamine seems to be excessive in patients with schizophrenia (and other psychotic disorders) and that medicines that block its activity can improve symptoms. Two other chemical messengers, norepinephrine and serotonin, may be out of balance in those with depression. Perhaps there are still others amiss in those we call psychopaths. Could the theater of Kappler's destructiveness have been as minute as the synapse, that joining place where one brain cell speaks to another in the language of chemical messengers?

Or was his future etched at birth on his chromosomes? One of Kappler's aunts reportedly died in a mental institution. Alcoholism plagued his parents. His mother reportedly drank during her pregnancy with him. A sister suffered with depression.

In provoking such questions, John Kappler's case embodies psychiatry's struggle to understand and treat the pathology in its domain. His illness emerged during years when powerful new medications were being used to control psychosis. Their availability apparently was helpful at times in restoring him to some measure of stability. But they may as well have aided in avoiding a definitive exploration of his life. Medication with no extensive insight-oriented psychotherapy and close monitoring may have been something akin to suturing shut a wound that still festers deep beneath the skin. When the pain relievers are stopped, the infection makes its progress known in no uncertain terms.

Jack Kehoe remembers a discussion he had with Frank Miller back at the Bowman Gray School of Medicine in the 1950s. He was arguing the merits of biological psychiatry; Miller advocated a more humanistic approach. After several minutes, Miller ended the conversation with a joke. "You think you're gonna cure Kappler with a pill?" he laughed.

Kappler's case also exposed the failings of psychiatry's diagnostic classifications. His mood and energy had plummeted twice, consistent with depression. His psychiatrist thought his paranoia and bizarre behavior seemed to fit more closely with a schizophrenic illness. And his personality and recklessness should have suggested psychopathy. Did he have three illnesses—or is there no technical diagnosis that truly encompassed his condition? And was it more important to give his disorder a name or to understand it?

For nearly a hundred years, psychiatry has been striving to apply medical model thinking to psychiatric disorders. In this model, the symptoms besieging patients are sorted into specific disease entities and the causes then identified and removed. For doctors of internal medicine, this works. In the case of diabetes mellitus, for example, the symptoms of urinary frequency, fatigue, and confusion often lead to suspicion of the underlying cause (a malfunctioning pancreas), which is confirmed by blood sugar monitoring and then treated by insulin replacement.

But psychiatric symptoms are much harder to sort into diagnoses. People with depression sometimes become paranoid. People with schizophrenia sometimes become depressed. Some people who hear voices have no other symptoms whatsoever, and others who hear voices also fall victim to terrible mood swings. Thus far, the hope that psychiatry would be able to identify homogeneous disease states, uncover the biological underpinnings, and remedy them has been largely a barren one.

Kappler's symptoms, however, evolved when the hope for psychiatry's becoming a true medical specialty was bright to the point of being blinding. Over the years he would collect over a dozen diagnoses and cavalierly take a myriad of medicines, but no one would be able to bring him close to confronting the past he had disowned, to stand a chance of making peace with it and, ultimately, overcoming it.

Several of the anesthesiology residents who trained with Kappler at the University of Southern California remember him as competent but easily moved to anger.

"He had the aura of having been on his own making decisions," one former resident, who wished to remain anonymous, reported. "When he had people making decisions and having authority over him, he had trouble. . . . He'd explode that this, that, or the other one didn't know anything."

"He didn't like to be told what to do by the surgeons," Dr. John Spence recalls. "He got into it with the surgeons."

Dr. Eva Henriksen, one of Kappler's instructors, noticed that he was unusually "concerned with order" and "uptight." "His mind was not 100 percent on anesthesia," she said.

But Kappler's demeanor and behavior apparently didn't cause anyone grave concern, possibly because there were other, more frightening doctors to contend with.

"Part of the problem in those days," said Dr. Ben Shwachman, who was a resident then, "was that nobody wanted to do anesthesia. We were listed as an economically depressed medical specialty. . . . It was a matter that the guy running the program literally needed bodies. He needed somebody to turn the gas on.

"Some of these people had severe problems. . . . It was a terrible time. . . . Anesthesia would take anybody. . . . People were crazy. If you were halfway decent you could write your own ticket. You could tell people to go to hell.

". . . A guy could have been a nut, but you'd tolerate him if he had any technical expertise. Who the hell was gonna replace him? You'd have guys jamming breathing tubes into the esophagus."

According to Dr. Henriksen, acceptance to the residency rested in the hands of one or two physicians. "There was no accountability to any committee or group of people," she said.

Supervision was spotty. There were too few full-time faculty members, and the part-time, voluntary faculty didn't always show up. "At the County [L.A. County Hospital] we had an enormous number of anesthesia residents," Dr. Richard Koons, a senior anesthesiologist in the 1960s, said. "The operating rooms were scattered in a hundred directions."

Dr. Bruce Bradley, a resident at that time, believes the USC department chairman, the late Dr. Sam Denson, knew of Kappler's psychiatric problems, but they may have paled in comparison to those of other trainees.

"There was one doctor who was down South," Bradley said. "He was shot by a security guard in a college dormitory. He came into the residency program after that and he started doing funny things. He finally tried to out-distance a patrolman who chased him for speeding. The patrolman shot him in the neck and killed him.

"There was another one two years ahead of me who hooked himself up to an IV drip of Brevital or Pentothal and didn't show up for work. He bumped himself off.

"A guy came from Arizona and blew his brains out.

"Another gal was told to finish her residency else-where. . . . She came back to the area, and some time in the middle sixties had a series of [patients who suffered] cardiac arrests while [she was] administering anesthesia. She was caught using Demerol ampules.

"There are a lot of them like this. . . . We had 're-treads'—people who had practiced in other fields and wanted to get out."

Dr. Maryanne Link, who also trained in anesthesia at USC in the 1960s, remembers one of her colleagues who "showed up at a hospital . . . with a gun and demanded Valium. She apparently had endometrial tissue [displaced tissue from the uterus] in her brain. She came with a good recommendation."

Kappler's recommendations and evaluations apparently aren't on file at USC anymore. Another of Kappler's in-structors searched for them. "The records are missing, for some reason," she said. "It's very unusual for us not to have the records."

Kappler finished his training in anesthesiology in 1968 and began working as a staff physician at St. Joseph's Medical Center in Burbank. But he shortly became a free-lancer with an anesthesiology service covering many area hospitals, because he was, said Tommie, uncomfortable with "hospital politics." Before his career ended, he would work in over fifty medical centers.

Being a freelance anesthesiologist afforded him a good deal of control over his environment and interpersonal relationships. He didn't have to get to know his patients and didn't have to fit in at any single hospital. Much of his day was spent in windowless operating rooms, gowned, gloved, and masked. His inner self was at a safe distance from the world.

He also had real power over people. He was a long way from being bullied in his back yard. His patients' lives were literally in his hands. He placed tubes in their throats and threaded them into their veins and arteries. He controlled their breathing and other vital functions. He took away their consciousness and restored it at will.

Still, he felt the need to remind others of his prominence, to build the walls thicker and higher around the Pittsburgh in him. "I was an extremely competitive specialist," he told psychologist Fred Kelso. "It was terribly important for me to be thought well of. There was no question I exaggerated my abilities and my knowledge."

In an attempt to put his colleagues on notice that his intellect was formidable, he frequently quoted data from obscure articles in medical journals, "a way of putting them down and at the same time elevating myself."

He set his fees relatively high, not so much because he needed the money as because he sensed that others would conclude that he was particularly skilled.

And again he was called "Dr. Kappler."

Dave Covell, who ran the anesthesiology service that got work for Kappler and did his professional billing, sensed that Kappler "was a person who had to be continually reassured by others that he was a worthwhile individual. He was easily offended. Somebody could make an offhand remark that he'd consider derogatory, and he'd be in the dumps. He was overly sensitive."

Even at home, Kappler wielded his professional identity like a shield. He couldn't risk exposure.

"I couldn't fool my wife," Kappler has said. "I would occasionally brag to her, but with my children, I played the over-worked, harassed physician."

Tommie tried to keep Dana, Kathryn, Elsie, Caroline, and the couple's infant, John F. Kappler III, from finding out that their father had suffered from psychosis. She treated him with medications herself, telling the children he had a bad cold or another physical illness and couldn't leave his room.

The house was full of secrets.

# CHAPTER 5

Things fall apart, the centre cannot hold,
Mere anarchy is loosed upon the world.

—W. B. Yeats

On November 23, 1975, Kappler's mask of sanity dropped.

Tommie saw her husband talking to himself during the afternoon and asked him if he was feeling well. He lied and assured her that he was fine.

The couple had dinner that night at Jean's Blue Room in Sherman Oaks. One of the other people dining there was an actress who had played a witch in *The Wizard of Oz*. Kappler began to wonder whether she might be a real witch.

His questioning of what was genuine and what was staged seems to have followed him into the night. He went to sleep, only to be awakened by voices that argued over who had ghostwritten Shakespeare's plays.

Psychiatric illnesses can recur without a clear stress, but Kappler's symptoms often had followed injuries to his self-esteem. Had something now happened to topple his fragile equilibrium? Was he facing financial trouble? Had his mother tried to reenter his life? Or was it simply that the weight of his armor finally felt that it might crush the little that was left of his core, true self? Perhaps the walls around his soul were beginning to feel inescapable, more like a prison than a fortress. As R. D. Laing has written: "This false-self system . . . can be regarded as an alien presence or person in possession of the individual. The 'self' has disavowed participation in it, the false-self system becomes enemy-occupied territory, felt to be controlled and directed by an alien, hostile, a destructive agency." The echoes of human pain denied become disembodied voices from beyond.

The voices were still speaking to him the next morning, instructing him to pick up hitchhikers on his way to work and to make a bizarre overture to an obstetrician who was a colleague. He peeked under the toilet stall that the obstetrician was using and reportedly asked, "Anything I can do for you?" Then he scrubbed and donned his surgical mask and gloves in preparation for anesthetizing a pregnant woman delivering by cesarean section. The voice told him to give her a variety of drugs, that she wasn't human, just a robot. Kappler listened and obeyed.

Dr. Ronald Travis, one of Kappler's colleagues working that day, remembers that the new mother suffered brain damage. The baby survived. Kappler then left the delivery suite to perform anesthesia on at least two other women. In both cases he signaled cardiac arrests, though none had occurred.

"I attempted to kill three patients . . . ," Kappler later told Dr. Kelso. "That was a very difficult thing for me to do. I was begging the voice not to make me do it—but I did it. . . . One presumes there is a reason. I don't question the reason. I know very little."

Amid the ensuing chaos, Kappler fled the hospital. He tried to break into a car in the parking lot but failed, then climbed into his own car and headed onto the freeway. The voice spoke again, he has said, and he complied with its direction, turning into the median strip while traveling at sixty to sixty-five miles per hour and striking another vehicle. When the occupants got out of their car, he stole it and drove into another accident. Finally he abandoned that car, too, and faced oncoming traffic, heeding the voices instructing him to jump in front of a bus. "I think the bus actually bumped me," he told Dr. Kelso. "I was directed, it was only a half-hearted effort on my part, because I found it so frightening."

This was to be only one of several half-hearted attempts by Kappler to kill himself. Suicide, it would seem, was more frightening to him than homicide.

He was arrested and spent several hours in a jail cell, where his bizarre behavior continued. He apparently tried to eat feces from a prison toilet bowl. Remembering Tommie's deceased brother, Dan, he sang "Danny Boy" to the police officers. He insisted on acting out a scene from *Romeo and Juliet* with an unwilling and enraged male inmate. Yet he was coherent enough to call Tommie and tell her where he was. She recruited three doctors from St. Joseph's to help post bail.

"He was just a mess," Tommie has said. "He had mucus—his hair was all wet. . . . He smelled like feces."

Inexplicably, she brought him home, not to a hospital. The children were told to stay in a back room with a neighbor, with the door closed. Kappler went into the bathroom.

"I went to the door and I heard him talking," Tommie has said, "and I asked him was he all right and he didn't answer me, but I kept hearing him talk. And he was shouting and calling out things and saying, 'Do I have to do it?' " He called out for God and Jesus. When Tommie opened the door she saw her husband with his head dipped into the toilet, drinking. He said he was doing a penance.

"It was full of feces," she has recalled. "He had diarrhea. He had been drinking it. . . . I flushed the toilet and came on out and realized how sick he was."

Tommie tried to clean him up, but he refused her ministrations.

Meanwhile, Kappler's three colleagues had called Burbank psychiatrist Lloyd Hyndman, who came to the Kappler home. Hyndman would be his psychiatrist for the next fifteen years, without keeping detailed notes on his treatment.

Hyndman decided to admit Kappler to the hospital by ambulance. When Kappler refused to go with the paramedics, the police were called to subdue him. Screaming obscenities and strapped to a stretcher, he was driven to the Glendale Adventist Hospital and admitted during the early morning hours. The doctor on call documented Kappler's "feverish activity, pressured thinking and speech, bizarre and irresponsible behavior and an element of grandiosity."

During the first few days of hospitalization Kappler defecated in his bedroom, remained unkempt, and occasionally drank from the toilets. He has said that he was conversing with dead relatives.

He was diagnosed this time as suffering from an acute manic psychosis, not schizophrenia. Mania, the flipside of depression, is an illness of mood in which patients have too much energy, often feel euphoric, and may grossly overestimate their abilities. Mania that alternates with depression is called bipolar disorder. Asked years later whether Dr. Kappler might have suffered from both schizophrenia and bipolar disorder, Dr. Hyndman's response revealed psychiatry's ill-conceived nosology. "No," Hyndman said. "Let me clarify. I never at any time considered Dr. Kappler to be schizophrenic or to be suffering from a schizophrenic disorder. Those two diagnoses [schizophrenia and bipolar disorder] are mutually exclusive. You either call it one or the other, but not both, although they overlap."

Kappler was again placed on antipsychotic medications. Although the medicines take weeks to alter significantly the brain chemical messengers at the root of psychosis, he seemed to improve quickly. Perhaps he was merely sedated by the drugs or contained by the structure and routine of the psychiatric ward. He was discharged December 10.

The discharge summary contained no mention of voices. "Dr. Kappler always told me he never heard voices," Dr. Hyndman stated much later. "In my initial hospitalization [progress notes on Kappler] I made reference to hallucinations in 1975. Dr. Kappler later corrected me and said, 'No, I don't hear voices. I never hear voices.'"

Kappler stayed at home ten days, then went back to work, freelancing again at many area hospitals. He never returned to St. Joseph's—another buried chapter in his life story—because he was embarrassed by what had happened there. When he wrote a resumé years later, he made no mention of the place, proudly stating that he had "always directed [my] efforts as a specialist towards excellence," had no malpractice suits against him, and had delivered anesthesia in over 1,000 surgeries.

There is no record that any of Kappler's colleagues from St. Joseph's—including those who knew of the multiple cardiac arrests in patients under his care and those who had seen him soaked and smelling of feces in jail—ever made any formal report to the state's Board of Medical Quality Assurance.

"There was, I remember . . . an emergency meeting, including the Chief of Staff," Kappler's colleague Dr. Travis recalls, "and he said, 'At times of crisis the best thing to do is calm down and wait a while before any decision.' Most of us came to his [Kappler's] defense. There were explanations for the three codes. If you're looking for that you can always find it. . . .

"It's a nightmare to get anyone out of practice, anyhow. In the back of our minds we probably wanted to avoid that."

Some physicians at St. Joseph's may have also wanted to avoid turning the spotlight on a colleague for fear it might one day be turned on them. Dr. Michael Greaney, chief of surgery at St. Joseph's at the time, suggested that other potential cases of malpractice might well have been covered up. "I'm one of those guys who knows where all the bodies are buried and who buried 'em," he said. "Everybody makes mistakes."

# CHAPTER 6

After that 1975 hospital admission, Tommie, who considered herself expert at detecting early signs of psychosis in her husband, would evaluate his stability every morning before he left for work. Later each day the two of them would speak by telephone so Tommie could make sure he was still rational. "When he's not right, there's a difference in the way he talks, and when I look at him, or hear his voice, I can spot it," Tommie told Dr. Kelso.

This arrangement gave Tommie tremendous responsibility for monitoring her husband's thinking and behavior. He had to check in with her, run things by her, satisfy her that he was well. In a way, she was the controlling mother he thought he had left behind in Pittsburgh.

When Kappler seemed to be getting sick, they lied to justify his absence from work, telling employers, friends, and even their own children that he had a cold or the flu. Then he would hide in his room at home, taking antipsychotic and mood-stabilizing medications until he seemed well.

Kappler had to bear the burden of his children's not knowing how fragile he was and his wife's refusing to acknowledge it. He had to pretend, just as he had as a boy, that he was strong and whole.

An individual with close ties to the Kappler family, who requested anonymity, described Tommie as obsessed with keeping her husband's illness hidden: "This is a woman who found keeping a secret more important than saving a life. She prides herself on keeping a secret, to the point that she allowed him to go to a hospital and work on patients in surgery. . . . She's a psychiatric nurse from hell."

A second person who knew the Kapplers well—and who, fearing retaliation by Tommie, also requested anonymity—recalled having seen Kappler in an obviously agitated state, angrily pacing back and forth without any clear provocation. "You're really frightening me," the individual remarked at the time. "What's the matter?"

"There's nothing wrong with him," Tommie shot back.

Yet another source expressed grave concern that Tommie might become enraged were any information about her or her family made public. "It's dealing with a person who's impossible," the individual explained. "I don't have words that would be adequate to describe her. . . . I know I was close enough [to John] that I should have been told [about his illness]. I should have been made aware. I never, ever was told."

Worse, Tommie's confidence in her clinical abilities seems to have been misplaced; she seemed ignorant about the management of psychiatric illness, believing for example, that the potent medication lithium (recommended to Kappler by Dr. Hyndman) was the equivalent of "a vitamin pill." She considered antipsychotic medications useful only during acute psychotic episodes, though it is widely accepted that they can prevent psychosis as well. Sometimes she didn't detect her husband's evolving symptoms until they had become severe and undeniable.

He was frequently able to conceal them from her.

"I was specifically chosen," Kappler explained later to court clinic psychiatrist Prudence Baxter. "A grand overall plan ran everything. Mine included the heavens and gods and the devil. It was exhilarating. The thing that was dangerous about it was that it was secret. I didn't blatherskite about it all over the street. The penalty for telling about it was death."

If forced to choose between his wife and the grand plan, in fact, Kappler said he would have chosen the latter. "If a voice told me to kill my wife . . . ," he told Dr. Kelso, "I certainly would want something more than that, some continued piece of instruction, so that I knew it wasn't some thought boiling up from within me. But I presume if I received some instruction[s] like that, that I would carry them out. Not without a certain amount of fear and concern that would have to be controlled and gathered, but I think I'm capable of doing that."

A year later, in 1976, Kappler was again hospitalized at Glendale Adventist. Tommie was with him at a church function when she "sensed" that he was confused. She called Dr. Hyndman and arranged for his admission the next day. The hospital records describe Kappler's symptoms as anything but subtle. He had become "sleepless," "anxiety-ridden," "paranoid," and "irritable" over the course of three days. His speech was unusually rapid.

He stayed in the hospital on medication just five days, returning to work again just a few weeks later.

According to Tommie, none of the many hospitals at which her husband worked was made aware that he had tried to harm patients at St. Joseph's. He continued to see Dr. Hyndman, sometimes every week, sometimes every other week, sometimes less than that. His use of medications was sporadic, though his recurrent psychotic episodes should have led him to use them regularly.

"During . . . '76 to '81, as I recall I saw him . . . irregularly," Hyndman stated in 1991. "In other words, he didn't keep appointments. He didn't want to take his lithium. He complained that he couldn't work while he was taking his lithium because of the side effects [including diarrhea and tremors], and it would interfere with his work. He would stop taking it and he wouldn't come in and see me. But I saw him periodically during those years."

At some point during 1976, Kappler stopped freelancing and joined the full-time anesthesiology staff at Hollywood Presbyterian Hospital in Los Angeles. Dr. Leon Robb, the Hollywood Presbyterian chairman of anesthesiology, hired him, over the objections of other staff anesthesiologists who, having heard about Kappler's day of cardiac arrests at St. Joseph's, were worried about his competence.

"Some of my colleagues said, 'You'd better not take him on. He's got a bad past—the bad seed,' " Robb told me. "I said, 'No. We'll just watch him. He's good.' " He knew that Kappler had had psychiatric difficulties but apparently never learned that they included making attempts on patients' lives. "I don't know the nature of his psychopathology, really," he admitted years later.

Besides, Kappler's recommendations were strong. Robb had received a very supportive letter of recommendation from Dave Covell of the Spring Anesthesia freelance group, the service that placed Kappler at hospitals during the late 1960s and 1970s. It made no reference to Kappler's problems, stating that he had established a reputation as competent, conscientious and very concerned about his patients. Covell had great confidence in him:

> He continues to be an exceedingly popular freelance Anesthesiologist, and I personally hold him in

the very highest esteem. Perhaps one of the best measures on an Anesthesiologist is, "Would you allow him to administer an anesthetic to you or to one of your family?" My answer is that I would unhesitatingly ask him to administer an anesthetic to me or any of my family at any time such services were necessary, regardless of the nature and/or severity of the surgery requiring such services. On a more personal basis, I would unhesitatingly recommend Dr. Kappler to the medical staff of any hospital as being a physician who would be an asset to that medical staff.

In addition, Robb had received a letter from Lloyd Hyndman, dated February 9, 1976, that confirmed Kappler was in continuing treatment with him. "Dr. Kappler is at this time," Hyndman wrote, "mentally stable and rational and fully competent to pursue professional objectives."

Robb did inquire of Kappler about what had occurred at St. Joseph's. "He told me he was exhausted and he had just broke," Robb said. "He basically just broke. He must have had the sub-soil to just lose it. . . . There were basically a series of mishaps."

Kappler had written Robb an extensive letter in which he apparently lied about the cases that had gone bad at St. Joseph's, reassuring him that they were simply difficult patients whom he had treated while overworked, deprived of sleep, and unsupported by colleagues. He made the point that his having left the full-time staff of St. Joseph's during 1974 had made the doctors and administration there resent him. Then he discussed the specific cases that had gone awry:

I had had insomnia for weeks. The night of the 22nd I slept hardly at all. I recall reaching a point around three AM when I knew it was too late to take a sleeping pill because of the morning responsibilities (my call started at 7 AM). The phone rang promptly at seven. I went to the OB unit at Saint Joseph's and found two women in labor. I put an epidural into one of them, then went to the delivery room on the run to care for the second. She was far advanced and refused spinal. The obstetrician planned to use forceps. I glanced at the chart and noted that she was allergic to Pentothal. Therefore, I mixed some Brevital and proceeded to induce. As I told you, she had an anaphylactic [allergic] response characterized first by an unobtainable blood pressure and then by EKG [electrocardiogram] changes. . . . The infant was delivered without difficulty, almost at the time of the induction. I was involved for the next hour and a half treating the shock, and myocardial response to it. I used steroids, Lidocaine, vasopressors, anti-histaminics. Finally, she was taken to the ICU. (Now Leon, I was upset not only because of the case itself, but also because the surgeon was clearly non-supportive. He had never cared for me dating back to a time when I had refused to do a case for him because of a low hemoglobin [blood oxygen]. There was a clear hostility. It sure didn't help the way I felt.)

I left the ICU to go to surgery where there was a bronchoscopy [lung examination] waiting. The patient was sixty-four going on eighty, smoked four packs a day, had a pO2 of around fifty [very low oxygen concentration in the blood] and, as I recall, had a grossly abnormal EKG with myocardial [heart muscle] damage prominent. On induction [of anesthesia] she threw a few PVC's [abnormal heartbeats], but seemed OK for the passage of the straight bronchoscope.

When Kappler inserted the bronchoscope, however, he noted that the patient still didn't seem to be getting enough oxygen. He took it out, but her heart started beating more and more abnormally, and she was taken to the intensive care unit.

The letter explained that Kappler's third patient that day was also a woman. After being anesthetized for an appendectomy, her heart began to beat in "a variety of weird rhythms." She was transported to the intensive care unit, as well.

Kappler invited Robb to share the information he was providing with hospital administrators, but asked him to be cautious with it. "I must consider each of the three cases as malpractice threats," he wrote, "though each did wuite [sic] well later; it is the legal record of these contents that concerns me."

One of Robb's special interests is in books by and about anesthesiologists who commit various crimes, including murder. He kept a file on Kappler, including the personal letters he received from him over the years. He sensed there was something extraordinary about him.

"He could blow up at the drop of a hat," Robb recalled. "I put my guts on the line for him, and he one time, in front of everyone, dressed me down something fierce. . . . He would rip a guy's tongue out if he did wrong."

On June 25, 1979, Kappler sent Robb a lengthy letter after being admonished by him in front of a younger anesthesiologist. The younger doctor had apparently complained about Kappler's taking a case himself that he felt should have been assigned to him. When confronted, Kappler had become angry, then tearful, prompting Robb to call Tommie with concerns about her husband's stability:

> Now, consider what happened Thursday. You were calm until I raised my voice. That embarrassed you in front of Gondol [the younger physician], to whose presence you had summoned me for discussion of his complaint, and your dentist friend. A face-saving response was necessary. You raised your voice until . . . I became teary-eyed. Done in again. Better call his wife, which just happens to be a neat way, if you haven't thought of it, to put me in my place for Sinning Against the Chief.

Kappler went on to describe how important a doctorly image was to him and how low his self-esteem could fall:

> . . . Now, consider some of the elements intrinsic to your summons to me, with Gondol present. Not only was your image of yourself on the line, but mine was too. No man I've ever seen works harder to maintain a high-class doctor's image than you, Leon; and though I go about it in different ways, I hope to be thought of respectfully, just like you. (I've paid a little dues in my time, and you only know the tip of the iceberg, though you might ask how you would be as a human being if you had tolerated my last five years [since the St. Joseph's cases]—years that began with zero self-respect. Part of the way I've come back is by reminding myself that *I have* been somebody. I was mentally healthy enough to get through medical school with respectable grades, working part-time, my wife working full-time, with our only daughter destined to die

during a sophomore year that was hell. We didn't ask a soul for help, as I had to ask you a few years back. That is who I was. And when Gondol was hardly born, I was a Sergeant First Class in Korea. Infantry. And I was, I like to recall, known as a pretty fine Chief Resident at County. The word was delivered to me that the Powers thought I was one of the finest they ever had. That is who I was.) So there it is. I'm not likely to chance losing face, because I need it to [*sic*] much. You have to see it melt to a complete blank before you can appreciate that kind of defensiveness. It isn't likely that I'll let anyone . . . talk down to me.

And, what of the tears? What chance does a fellow like me have if he can't avoid those situations in which image is at stake?

"He had a horrible, horrible temper—screaming, ranting, raving," Dr. Marshall Sands, another Hollywood Presbyterian anesthesiologist, confirmed. "He felt that if you criticized him, you were saying he was incompetent. . . . He used to get more angry as he vented his anger. . . . It was really something to watch. There were many times I felt he might get physical."

Kappler's explosiveness, however, still wasn't considered dangerous in a field that routinely embraced doctors with a range of problems.

"I have seen doctors absolutely lose it," Robb said. "We had one guy sniffing halothane [an anesthetic], and I had to pick him up off the floor. Another guy was injecting himself with narcotics. The patient would be awake; he'd just give a spinal and stick the vials [of general anesthetic] in his pocket. I saw him years later practicing in New York."

# CHAPTER 7

One day during 1980, according to Kappler, the darkest of his demons returned. He injected a patient with a lethal dose of the anesthetic Xylocaine.

"I can't recall if there was an auditory hallucination [a voice] or not," Kappler would tell Dr. Ebert. "I went out and got Xylocaine and injected it into the patient. Caused a cardiac arrest. We resuscitated her. There was no damage."

Kappler called Tommie at home. He sounded upset and confused.

"Stay where you are and I'll come pick you up," she directed him. Again, rather than bringing him to a hospital, she brought him home.

Asked whether she ever told anyone at Hollywood Presbyterian about her husband's homicidal behavior, Tommie would respond, "I don't think the hospital ever knew. Nothing happened to the patient, you understand. There was no problem. It was just something he did."

For the next two months, under the guise of having hepatitis, he stayed in his room, taking antipsychotic medication prescribed by Dr. Hyndman and given to him by his wife.

Then he went back to work.

Dr. William Casey, a urologist who performed surgery on patients anesthetized by Kappler, remembers him vividly. He recalls Kappler's giving a lecture about anesthesia to the staff and becoming inexplicably enraged, nearly to the point of screaming about the subject. When he later asked Kappler the reason for his outburst, he found him oddly unaware that he had acted strangely at all.

"I always wondered what the content of his thought might be," Casey said. "I wondered if he was hearing voices." Casey recalled that Kappler would sometimes interrupt surgery that seemed to be going quite well. "On several occasions he [Kappler] said, 'You've got to stop the operation, the patient's not going to make it.' But he seemed so angry. . . . It sends a chill through me."

At the moment Kappler injected Xylocaine into his patient, was he acting by choice? Even if he was not shackled to abnormal chromosomes or an abnormal brain, was he a prisoner, nonetheless, of his early experiences, captive to an inescapable life story? When does a man own his face?

These are not new questions. They have been the domain of law, morality, and religion for all time. They are the core of Camus' Mersault and Dostoevsky's Raskolnikov. St. Thomas Aquinas and Gandhi found in them the foundations for viewing sin as its own punishment and crime as illness.

Psychiatry itself is unsure where to draw the line separating illness, aberrance, and depravity. The field's official diagnostic manual lists not only major mental illnesses, like depression and schizophrenia, but eleven separate disorders of personality, or character, among them, antisocial (psychopathic) personality disorder, narcissistic (self-centered) personality disorder, and paranoid (suspicious) personality disorder.

Yet patients diagnosed with these enduring—and sometimes very destructive—ways of relating to others are not generally accorded the full sick role and do not inspire pure sympathy from caretakers. Assumed to have some control over their symptoms, they often spark an uncomfortable mixture of reluctant compassion and frank anger. Such ambivalent feelings can be stirred by patients with any personality disorder, but it is a very common reaction to those diagnosed with *antisocial personality disorder*, whose symptoms include lawlessness, lying, and lack of empathy for others. Many psychiatrists who diagnose and treat them believe that these people are bad, not sick, and should be the responsibility of the criminal justice system.

Unfortunately, the field of psychiatry has shied away from grappling with such philosophical and moral dilemmas, though they are part of every psychiatrist's work. In its zeal to mimic objective science, it has all but ignored the crucial subjective issues inherent in any attempt to change patients' lives.

It has lost sight of the soul while looking in microscopic detail at the brain.

Kappler struggled with the subjective questions himself. Schooled as he was in medicine, knowing what he did about illnesses like depression, mania, and schizophrenia, he still wondered whether the voices he heard might be those of the devil. "I'm willing to accept that the devil is God," he told Dr. Kelso.

And if his problem was with evil, he seemed uncertain whether the dark force was alien to him or part of him. He wondered at times whether the voices reflected his core feelings. He told Dr. Kelso they might represent "an over-inflated self," that they came from inside (rather than outside) his head, and that they may have been with him even as a child. Asked by Kelso whether he considered himself psychotic when hearing voices, Kappler reportedly replied, "I don't know the answer to that. I can't tell you that. It's an extremely seductive relationship."

He sometimes had difficulty sorting out whether the voice had given him complete instructions or provided just the seed of an idea, which he then enlarged upon himself.

According to forensic psychologist J. Tyler Carpenter, who examined him after Paul Mendelsohn's murder, Kappler indicated that the voice that had instructed him to drive onto the jogging path in Cambridge "could have been his own voice," that perhaps he was, in a way, talking to himself. Yet Dr. Hyndman insists Kappler consistently denied hearing voices at all.

Defending against the specter of evil inside him may have been one of Kappler's motivations for working as an usher in church (even though he was not a religious man), working in church-affiliated hospitals, and making a good deal of the fact that he was no lineage to a Nazi war criminal who shared his name.

What Kappler apparently couldn't bear—or chose not to—was to examine that darkness in him, to be rid of what he had suffered in Pittsburgh finally by looking at it rather than running away from it.

Was this failure to do so in and of itself evil, or was it testimony to an infirmity of character—an anemia of the ego—caused by psychological injuries sustained as a child? Does the fact that Kappler returned to medical practice after nearly killing patients prove a kinship with the devil? Or does it prove how terrified he was of complete annihilation without the insulating authority of his profession?

John A. Sanford, writing on the legend of Dr. Jekyll and Mr. Hyde, identifies this failure to acknowledge and explore one's dark side—one's shadow as Jung called it—as the fuel for destructiveness: "Henry Jekyll's fundamental mistake was his desire to escape the tension of the opposites within him. . . . He was gifted with a modicum of psychological consciousness, more than most men, for he knew that he had a dual nature; he was aware that there was another one in him whose desires were counter to his more usual desires for the approbation of mankind. Had he enlarged this consciousness and carried the tension of the opposites within him, it would have led to the development of his personality; . . . he would have been individuated. But Jekyll chose instead to try to escape this tension by means of the transforming drug, so that he could be both Jekyll and Hyde and have the pleasures and benefits of living out both sides of his personality without guilt or tension. For as Jekyll, it is worth noting, he felt no responsibility for Hyde. 'For it was Hyde, after all, and Hyde alone that was guilty,' he once declared."

# FIRST PERSON

Some months after we had talked by telephone, I flew from Boston to visit Leon Robb in North Hollywood. He had been reticent to share everything he knew about John Kappler—including the content of the letters he had received from him—until he could meet me personally and be reassured that I was "legitimate."

Robb's pain clinic, which occupies a suite on the second floor of a drab office building, is something of a family business. Robb's wife, Carole, keeps the books, and his son practices physical therapy there.

Robb himself is a silver-haired man of great confidence, with a voice that is a near duplicate of Kasey Kasem's. He is the kind of doctor whose presence inspires ready trust from patients, one of the reasons he has been able to build a thriving multisite practice.

I found Robb friendly and warm and felt comfortable sitting in his private conference room to review the thin file he had kept on John Kappler for two decades. He seemed instantly comfortable with me, too. Although I presented no credentials, I must have seemed legitimate enough to merit his further confidence.

More than once while researching this book, I had been

taken aback by how willing so many people were to share what they remembered about John Kappler. I had expected that the passage of so many years and the lack of contact with Kappler would make it relatively easy for his childhood friends, high school classmates, and even college classmates to speak openly about him. But I had anticipated more of an allegiance of silence from the medical students, residents, and fellow physicians with whom he had trained and worked.

Once I identified myself as a doctor, however, dozens of physicians shared their stories about Kappler's temper and peculiarities. They freely told tales of chaos in a number of hospitals, of doctors anesthetizing patients while on drugs themselves, of dangerous physicians vagabonding state to state with no intervention by their colleagues.

I heard these things in at least two different ways. The physician in me was warmed by the trust extended to me as an insider; the journalist in me was fascinated by the number and depth of dark revelations. The disparity between the ways of listening created other emotions: I felt both excited and guilty about playing the role of a participant-observer, a double agent of sorts in the house of medicine. I sensed that many of my sources considered me—by virtue of my medical degree—the most sympathetic of biographers. But I knew that an objective book would leave some of them thinking me a traitor.

Even hospital publicity departments, Kappler's medical school, and medical professional societies helped with my research. After I introduced myself as a doctor, none asked the specific focus of my book. (Not all doctors consented to be interviewed. When they refused, I felt not only disappointed but unfairly shut out of the inner circle.)

My sense of being both an insider and an outsider was heightened by the fact that I have basked in the brotherhood of medicine myself. I have enjoyed the camaraderie that makes off-color jokes acceptable during twenty-four-hour shifts. I have laughed with a surgeon friend who recounted how he had become enraged with a nurse and thrown a tray of instruments across the operating room. I even know of one impaired physician who continues to practice today. I have never formally reported him.

How much of that tolerance for potential injury to patients, I wonder now, is anger cloaked in brotherhood? Is there an element of low self-esteem in most doctors that fuels the desire to be in authority and control? Could the desire to heal be in part an imperfect psychological defense against the desire to harm?

Robb joined me between patients to answer questions his file on Kappler raised and to provide what recollections he could to put the material in context. Until later in my visit, he didn't know that Kappler had told forensic experts in Massachusetts about having tried to kill several patients, including the three at St. Joseph's and another at Hollywood Presbyterian.

Robb said he hired Kappler because he felt he was an able and principled anesthesiologist who had had a run of bad luck—combined with exhaustion—at St. Joseph's. Kappler appealed to Robb's vision of himself as a healer. "I feel badly for people when I feel they have quality and don't get a fair deal," he explained. "He [Kappler] had ethics and he had morals."

Because he had gone out on a limb to hire Kappler, he was particularly aggrieved by the other man's repeated verbal and written attacks on him. On one occasion, Kappler walked into the operating room where Robb was performing anesthesia and began to confront him about a perceived injustice. He smelled of alcohol.

"I pushed him against the wall," Robb said, "and told

him we'd talk about the whole thing in a more appropriate setting.''

Two years later, on April 1, 1981, Kappler distributed a memo to the anesthesiology staff that was highly critical of Robb for building a lucrative private practice that changed his availability to the hospital-based group practice.

No one forced Dr. Leon Robb into the rigors of an office practice; it was a purely personal choice, and it was almost certainly based upon the expectation— certainly realized by now—that he could earn more at two jobs than one. (There is no reason to think it is missionary work being done in the Tower. There is every reason to believe that a probably very generous income is being generated for each afternoon's labor and the bleatingly offered complaints of short calls, while ignoring the massive logistical accommodation [sic] already made by the group, might come from inside something other than a sheep's skin.)

I think the time has come for Dr. Robb to be welcomed back into the fold of the present reality. If he wishes to be a part of the group, let him abide by the professional concerns and peer-respecting scheduling methods of group members. He has the option of practicing totally outside the group, scheduling himself from his office. We have the option of letters like this one, intra-group scheduling pressures, or appeals to committees, etc., external to the anesthesia staff. The inviting in of outside people to solve problems within our group tends to have unfavorable long-term effects, suggesting as it would, that we or our elected officers are impotent.

A handwritten notation underneath Kappler's signature at the end of the letter read: "Indicates animosity & Resentment. Perhaps Some Jealousy."

I took the time between Robb's chats with me to look at the art adorning the conference room walls. They were caricatures. One, labeled "Neurolytic," portrayed a patient with a huge needle and syringe stuck into his back. The syringe was being filled by a dump truck emblazoned with the words "A to Z Toxic Waste." Another, labeled "Spinal Stimulation," showed a lightning bolt striking a patient. A third was a comic drawing of Robb's wife Carole standing next to him at a desk covered with money bags, demanding that he "Keep It Coming!"

Robb later showed me, with great enthusiasm, a textbook on anesthesia he had saved that was written by convicted murderer Dr. Carol Coppolino. Coppolino had injected his wife with the untraceable paralytic agent succinylcholine, frequently used during surgical procedures. Robb had tucked the article on Coppolino's conviction inside the cover of the book.

After I told Robb that Kappler had indeed tried to kill patients, he seemed genuinely moved. "So I could have hired a killer, then?" he asked, incredulous. "I may have given a killer access to patients?" The possibility jogged Robb's memory of other calamities involving Kappler.

"I was giving anesthesia one day," Robb said, "and I noticed I was done and I turned the oxygen on, and the kid wasn't waking up.... The kid had a transient [cardiac] arrest. We resuscitated him. I couldn't figure out what the hell was wrong."

When Robb examined the machine being used to deliver the anesthesia, he realized the problem: "The shut-off valve became defective, so when you switched to pure oxygen it became pure anesthetic. John Kappler had used the same machine [on the case preceding Robb's], and the patient had died. Anesthesia machine number 5 in room 9.'' According to Robb, the hospital was to investigate the problem with the machine, but the defective valve disappeared.

In another case, he recalled, the pump reservoir of the machine Kappler was using blew up, shutting down the flow of oxygen and killing the patient.

Robb looked at me excitedly, suddenly gripped by a new realization. "I could have been in danger, then," he said. He called his wife in to join us. "Honey, if what he's saying is true," he sparkled, "I could easily have been a target of a killer, without even knowing it."

# CHAPTER 8

During 1981, one of the Kapplers' daughters was considering joining the Peace Corps, and the couple visited the home of Pam White, a Hollywood Presbyterian nurse who had served in the Corps herself.

Kappler's paranoia was brewing: He had told Tommie that he was concerned their daughter was involving herself with spies and that White might be checking out the family. Nonetheless, Tommie accompanied her husband to White's home to watch slides of her overseas experiences. After they returned, Tommie has said, "he seemed to be very preoccupied or upset about seeing the slides and [he was] suggesting that she was a member of an intelligence group." He became extremely agitated, to the point that Tommie saw him angrily pacing in the upstairs bedroom and talking to himself. She finally called Dr. Hyndman and her father-in-law, who was living just a few miles away.

When his father came to the house, Kappler insisted that Tommie and her father-in-law make love in front of him.

"My husband wanted my father-in-law and myself to go up and have sexual intercourse, and he was going to watch," Tommie has said. "Well, he became insistent on it, and so I went and called our friend who is an Episcopal minister, and asked him to come over. . . . Then I went back into the living room and told my husband that our friend was coming over, and that we wouldn't have time to go up and do anything. He became a little forceful, and said that, well, we were going to have to go up and do this."

With the minister's help, Tommie was able to get her husband admitted again to the Glendale Adventist Medical Center. Once there, he reported hearing voices and rated his own clarity of thought as brilliant. Many of the ideas he expressed revolved around his wish to be dominant and in control. A document signed by Dr. Hyndman notes "auditory hallucinations"—voices.

As had been the case before, Kappler's symptoms seemed to yield readily to medications. He stayed at the hospital just four days.

The hospital discharge summary noted that Kappler had been "working and functioning well up until the day prior to hospitalization." His outpatient medications were to include the mood stabilizer lithium and the antipsychotic medication Haldol.

Although Tommie reportedly knew that her husband had been hearing voices, she never notified Hollywood Presbyterian of that fact. He returned to work there about two weeks later.

For the next three years, Kappler was on and off medication. He didn't like the side effects of lithium or Haldol, which include not only diarrhea and hand tremors but also stiffness and twitching. Some patients also object to feeling controlled by psychoactive medications, anchored too firmly to a reality in which they are not special or all-powerful.

When his psychiatric symptoms worsened, Kappler was treated at home, not in the hospital.

Dr. Hyndman, who continued to see Kappler as an outpatient, would later say that the couple withheld information from him, sometimes choosing not to report psychotic episodes. Still, medical records indicate that he failed to adequately document the presence and level of medication in Kappler's blood, data he could have obtained through routine blood tests.

In 1984, Tommie took the children on a trip to Mexico. Before leaving, she worried that her husband seemed confused. He was smiling strangely, and she thought he might be talking to himself again. But after consulting with Dr. Hyndman (by her report), she left anyway. She didn't tell the hospital of her concerns, and Kappler went to work.

At the end of a long day, he has said, he started to hear voices again. As he got in his car, "a voice said, 'You're going to kill yourself in an automobile accident. You have to do this. There is no choice,' " he later told Dr. Ebert. "And there was a threat in this for my family. I had to do it or my family would suffer. The voice said, 'You're really not going to die, you're going to reappear in Ireland as a potato farmer.' "

Kappler sped down a street near his home. Rather than barreling into a tree or an unoccupied vehicle, he accelerated to (by his estimation) between sixty-five and eighty miles per hour and drove straight for the back of a car with a young woman in it.

"She wasn't hurt at all," Kappler later said. "It was amazing. I went through the windshield, sustained a fracture of my sternum. They had to pull me out of the car. Tomy [*sic*] flew in the next day. She realized I was psychotic. I thought the nurse [in the hospital] was my Irish wife, and I reached over and grabbed her on the breast.''

Kappler says he created a cover story to conceal his violent intent, telling the insurance company he had simply fallen asleep at the wheel.

He apparently told the police a different story, however. ''I was on Coldwater . . . when my gas pedal stuck and [the car] accelerated faster and faster out of control,'' a police report from 1984 quotes him as saying. ''It is a new car. I can't understand why it happened. The gas pedal has never stuck before. I really didn't notice V-2 [police abbreviation for the second car] until about impact. My chest and head hurt.''

After about a week in the medical unit of Riverside Hospital, Kappler went home with Tommie rather than to a psychiatric unit. He was back at Hollywood Presbyterian within a month or so, administering anesthesia daily, often in cases of open heart surgery. He worked twenty-four-hour shifts on the obstetrical service and the trauma service, as often as twice a week.

Tommie called the hospital to check on him four times a day.

# CHAPTER 9

Kappler's anesthesia career finally ended on April 29, 1985. Nurse Patricia Shea had called to ask him to look in on a quadriplegic patient, Ben Wytewa, who was a friend of her sister. Wytewa had attempted suicide and was in the intensive care unit of Hollywood Presbyterian on a respirator.

Kappler was on twenty-four-hour trauma call. When he had left for work on April 28, "he seemed to have a little strange look in his eyes, and his voice seemed funny to me," Tommie has said. "And I asked him was he all right. He said, 'Fine.' And he went to work." Tommie checked in with him four times during the day and evening and felt reassured that he was well.

But at about 10:45 P.M. on April 28, approximately fifteen minutes after Tommie's final call, Wytewa's respirator was turned off. A nurse in his room could identify the culprit only as a man wearing hospital scrubs, who had glasses like Kappler's. When the respirator fell silent, the nurse called for help, and the patient was stabilized.

Kappler, who had been seen staring at Wytewa hours before the unplugging and hours after it, was arrested in the early morning of April 29, after performing anesthesia on another surgical patient.

He called Tommie from jail at about 7:00 A.M. She visited with him, then, by her report, called Dr. Hyndman to tell him that the voices had told her husband to turn the respirator off.

Kappler was released on $10,000 bail later that day. Rather than taking him to a psychiatric facility, Tommie treated him with the antipsychotic Haldol at home.

Paul Feldman of the *Los Angeles Times* covered the story on May 14:

## DOCTOR ACCUSED OF CUTTING OFF PATIENT'S LIFE SUPPORT SYSTEM

A Van Nuys physician was charged with attempted murder on Monday for allegedly removing, without authorization, the life support system of a brain-damaged patient at Hollywood Presbyterian Medical Center.

Dr. John Federick Kappler, 55, an anesthesiologist who has been on the hospital staff since 1972, is accused of turning off the respirator used to keep Ben Wytewa alive in the medical center's intensive care unit.

Wytewa, a 28-year-old Los Angeles electrician, has been hospitalized since apparently attempting suicide last January by jumping out of a window of his residence. Authorities said the alleged murder attempt occurred on April 29 in a room containing several patients whose breathing was being assisted by respirators.

When an alarm went off after the device was unplugged, a nurse in the room quickly responded and restored Wytewa's breathing manually and also rang for assistance, Morrison Chamberlin, chief executive officer of the 389-bed hospital, said.

## Witnesses Saw Suspect

Authorities said that Kappler had apparently looked in on the patient at least once before allegedly turning off the respirator. Witnesses saw Kappler entering and exiting the room at the time the machine was turned off, district attorney's office spokesman Al Albergate said. After the incident, Kappler went to another part of the hospital to help perform a surgery, according to Albergate. Kappler was arrested in the hospital about seven hours after the episode by police officers who had been contacted by the hospital security force.

Wytewa suffered no unusual complications and his condition remains guarded, Chamberlin said.

Since Wytewa cannot speak, he has not been interviewed by police, said Lt. Charles Vassey of the Police Department's Northeast Division.

Police have not yet determined a motive.

"That's the $64,000 question," Massey said.

## Kappler Suspended

Chamberlin said that Kappler has been suspended from the staff pending resolution of the case.

Kappler, reached in Van Nuys on Monday, refused to comment on the case. He is free on $10,000 bail pending his arraignment, scheduled for Thursday. If convicted, the physician faces up to nine years in state prison, authorities said.

Kappler's lawyer, William A. Francis, said that his client had been in the room of the patient on the evening of April 29, but "I'm positive he did not consciously turn off the respirator."

Francis said that Kappler "feels very, very distressed by the charges."

The attorney said that, according to police reports, two nurses were in the room when a man walked in and turned off the respirator. He said that, according to the report, one nurse could not identify the man and the other one did not see the incident.

A source close to the investigation said that the state Board of Medical Quality Assurance had reported no prior complaints against Kappler.

Echoed Massey: "To the best of our knowledge—and we've investigated the thing for two weeks—this is an isolated incident peculiar to this time and place."

Massey said Kappler was not Wytewa's doctor and that their only relationship was that Kappler had reviewed Wytewa's medical chart, apparently at the request of a distant associate who knew a friend of Wytewa.

At his hearing in June, Kappler pleaded innocent to the crime. His lawyer told *Los Angeles Times* reporters covering the highly publicized case, "He's very distressed by what's going on. Right now he's affected in that he doesn't have hospital staff privileges, so he cannot practice his craft."

No one could positively identify Kappler, and the charges against him were dismissed.

Paul Feldman reported on the judge's decision on June 12:

## DOCTOR FREED OF ATTEMPTED MURDER COUNT

A charge of attempted murder was dismissed Tuesday against Dr. John Frederick Kappler, a Van Nuys physician whom authorities had accused of removing, without authorization, the life-support system of a brain-damaged patient at Hollywood Presbyterian Medical Center last April.

Los Angeles Municipal Judge Edward L. Davenport dismissed the charge after a two-day preliminary hearing in which prosecutors were unable to provide witnesses who could positively identify Kappler as having been in the hospital room of patient Ben Wytewa when his respirator was turned off. Wytewa was stabilized by nurses and suffered no unusual complications.

"I'm just very relieved," said Kappler, 55, tears flowing from his eyes, as he and his wife, Tommie, left the courtroom.

However, the thin, graying anesthesiologist, who has worked at Hollywood Presbyterian for more than a decade, added that his future remains uncertain. The charges, he said, have scarred his reputation and altered the working climate at the hospital, where he was suspended from the staff pending resolution of the case.

"The mere fact that the charge was levied," Kappler said, "(means) that if anything happens in a hospital and I don't have an alibi, I'm screwed."

Deputy Dist. Atty. David P. Conn had no immediate reaction on whether the case will be dropped, appealed or refiled.

"I can't say this was expected," Conn said, "and I can't say this was unexpected. I can say we just put all the evidence on that we had." . . .

In making his decision, Davenport said, "The description [provided by the nurse in Wytewa's room] could fit anybody."

The fact that Kappler was in the vicinity was not conclusive, the judge added, since Kappler worked in the building. Additionally, no proof was offered by prosecutors, he said, of Kappler's intent to commit murder.

"I suppose the only motive (he could have had) was he wanted to put this person out of his misery," Davenport mused. "It's a little bizarre he kept bouncing into that room. (But) maybe he's (just) a strange and bizarre person."

*Witness Presented*

Defense attorney William A. Francis presented no evidence on Kappler's whereabouts at the time of the incident. However, he did present a witness to explain why Kappler had entered the room on the other occasions.

Patricia Shea, a former nurse at Hollywood Presbyterian, said she had called Kappler that day and asked him to check on Wytewa's condition as a favor to her sister, who was a friend of Wytewa.

Outside the courtroom, the relieved Kappler, still wiping away tears, questioned the prosecutor's case.

"If I had done it," he said, "obviously I would never have gone back in the damn room."

Asked where he was at the time of the incident, Kappler said, "I was in the john in Room 426" (a room set aside at Hollywood Presbyterian where doctors working long hours can rest).

The case was never refiled, but Kappler became increasingly depressed, and finally he retired. "It was reasonable for me to get out because of the publicity," he told Dr. Ebert. "It was impossible for me to practice after that once the cloud of suspicion . . . you can't do it, so I retired on Social Security disability. Now I'm on Medicare."

The automatic respect that went with his medical degree, colleagueship with physicians, authority over nurses, affluence, even the opportunity to control the vital functions of patients, were all gone. His armor had been stripped away. Anyone who cared to look deeply enough could have seen the Pittsburgh in him. He was exquisitely vulnerable, utterly alone.

In response to a standard question about personal grooming needs on his Medicare disability application, Kappler reported, "I did grow a beard when this all started so that I wouldn't be recognized."

He would dine publicly only with specific people he trusted.

Elsewhere on the application he noted, "My wife says my mind wanders when I drive."

According to Leon Robb, Kappler decided to work for a time after the 1985 incident at a free clinic in the valley. The clinic called Robb, he said. "I didn't say a thing to them about his emotional problems. Here's a guy who loves medicine and wants to practice. I'm not going to stand in his way.''

Dr. Hyndman let Kappler's visits with him dwindle to monthly sessions, then bimonthly. He often let Kappler order his own medicines through a supply house rather than writing him prescriptions to be filled by and monitored at a pharmacy. During 1986, he wrote to an insurance company, ''It is conceivable that at some point in the distant future, perhaps years from now, Dr. Kappler may be able to undertake some work as a physician. At this point even that seems unlikely.''

At a deposition after Paul Mendelsohn's death, Hyndman was asked what efforts he had made, other than talking with Kappler, to confirm the details of the 1985 incident involving Ben Wytewa. ''Well, none,'' was his answer. ''That's not my business.''

# PART THREE

# FINAL JOURNEY

# CHAPTER 10

For the Truth is past all commiseration.

—Maxim Gorky

After leaving Los Angeles for Boston in 1990, Kappler drove alone about six days, staying in cheap motels on the way to Alabama where Tommie was flying to join him. The increasing distance from his wife may have stressed his fragile ego. Twice before when travel had separated the two of them, he had ended up being admitted to psychiatric hospitals.

By the time Tommie arrived at the airport, Kappler remembers that he was already beginning to have bizarre thoughts. Tommie told him that she had been seated next to the musical arranger for Ray Charles on the plane; he took the comment as a sign that he would be led out of his own blindness, allowed to see things that had been hidden from him.

What did John Kappler think would be revealed to him? Was the notion of his own blindness a random and inexplicable delusion? Or can it be understood as a sign that the vulnerable and injured parts of himself were so deeply buried that he could experience them now only as unfathomable vibrations of his soul, dark secrets kept even from him?

"This process has always been an insidious and seductive one," he told Dr. Ebert months later. "I've never been able to determine at any point that I was beginning to think dangerously. I just little by little found myself in the psychotic state.''

Visiting friends and relatives in Alabama, Florida, South Carolina, and North Carolina after meeting up with Tommie meant facing not only memories of their child who had died of cancer but evidence of the death of his dreams for himself.

"In some ways," Kappler has said, "I retired in disgrace. Here are people I admired and loved, and they were still working."

Kappler's routine after retirement had consisted largely of going to movies, hiking, shopping, taking care of the house, and reading. He had picked up biking as a hobby, but when a close friend had been killed in a bicycle accident, he had stopped riding. The volunteer work he had tried, said Tommie, was "not very ego rewarding." At one point he had tried to get a job in the insurance industry but may have been undermined by the depressions that visited him repeatedly.

"Because he was on this disability," Tommie told Dr. Kelso, "he really couldn't make much money." She remembers her husband being particularly disturbed en route to Boston when the couple went boating on a friend's yacht. "Look at what we don't have," he told her.

Perhaps he felt the Pittsburgh churning in him, threatening to boil onto the surface for everyone to see. There was no way he could deny the cheap motels he stayed in on his solo drive, no way to disguise the Hyundai, no pat answer as to why one of the intellectual leaders of the Bowman Gray class of 1960 should have ended up, in Kappler's own words, a "house husband."

The couple reached Washington, D.C., on April 7. There was life all around them. Cherry blossoms were carried everywhere by the spring breeze. Their daughter Dana and her husband, Brooke, who lived in nearby Arlington, Virginia, had given them a grandchild.

But there was no peace in Washington for John Kappler. The injury to his self-esteem was driving him into his dark domain of demons, a world in which he was special and powerful. Tommie was becoming the direct focus of his paranoia.

The two of them had coffee at their motel in Washington, D.C., one morning and met a man who spoke with them about some of the other cities he had visited.

"I began to have the feeling," Kappler told Dr. Kelso, "he was speaking directly to me, even though he was describing experiences of his own from the past."

When the man mentioned the town of Exeter in New Hampshire, Kappler focused on that word as an encoded message to him to "exit her," meaning Tommie. He thought he might be receiving instructions to kill her.

"It was very frightening to me," Kappler recalled. ". . . If that were the case, there would be instructions down the road—it was only the vaguest reference, I don't know. Conceivably I misunderstood this guy, I don't know. . . . Just the mere fact that I would be responsible for her death frightened me."

The words "exit her," taken literally, testify to the extent Kappler may have felt enveloped, suffocated, and, in the worst way, mothered by his wife.

Tommie noticed that her husband hardly touched his food as they chatted with the other man, and he had a strange look on his face. She asked him if everything was all right.

"Oh, yes," he assured her.

As so often in the past, Kappler had no intention of making Tommie privy to his thoughts. "I was not permitted to share this with her," he told Dr. Ebert. "Only

*I* have been chosen. There never has been any discussion with others.''

Tommie didn't bring him to an emergency room or insist that he take antipsychotic medication.

As they drove to New Jersey, Kappler reportedly believed people in other cars could read his mind and that fellow travelers at restaurants along the way might be trying to give him additional messages.

They spent a night at a motel in New Jersey that was convenient to the Pathfinder train into Manhattan.

"I had the feeling on that train," Kappler has said, "that I was being watched, that people knew who we were, and somehow were paying homage."

His sense of being well-known and extraordinary was heightened when a black girl and a Hispanic man gave him and his wife directions to and from the city. "As you know," he told Dr. Kelso, "New York isn't famous for courtesy. I thought it was rare. I felt as if, perhaps, they were directed to do what they were doing and say what they were saying."

During the visit to Manhattan, Jack noticed that his father seemed unusually tired and slowed. He shared his concerns with Tommie, but she still didn't get Kappler professional help.

The Kapplers arrived in the Boston area on April 11 to stay with their daughter, Elsie, in nearby Medford.

A poster of Suleiman the Magnificent, sultan of Turkey during the sixteenth century, hung outside Elsie's bedroom where the couple slept.

"I felt as if that meant I had to sully [to soil] myself, that I would be sullied," Kappler told Dr. Ebert. "I thought that throughout I had been sullied in 1985 and I would be sullied further. My name would be sullied. I thought of that poster a lot. I kept thinking have I not sullied myself enough? When does the sullying stop? The voices said it will get worse before it gets better.''

On a visit to downtown Boston, Kappler believed that a stranger who gave him and Tommie directions might have a special relationship with her. "I began to feel like a dog she was dragging around," he told Dr. Kelso. "She's an attractive person, and I was kind of an old, bearded guy."

"I kept having this thought," he went on, "that she, that she was . . . you know, normally, in our relationship, in my mind, I always figure I'm as smart as she is. . . . I began to feel that she knew so much more. . . . I got the feeling that she had some kind of kinship with these people that I did not have . . . it was just a matter of intellect. I began to feel very inferior."

In what may have been an attempt to defend against such feelings of worthlessness and reestablish a measure of self-esteem, Kappler gave money away to each homeless person he saw. Tommie had to stop him from offering a handout to one woman who didn't seem to be homeless at all.

But even when Kappler woke in the middle of the night and mumbled something about needing to take some medicine, Tommie still didn't get him to a psychiatrist.

The next day the couple toured the coastal town of Rockport together. At a pier, they walked past an impressive-looking, uniformed army officer who seemed to stare at them. Kappler felt that the officer was delivering a message to him, telling him that he would have to be just as stalwart in the days ahead.

He perused a biography of Andrew Jackson at a local bookshop and read of a duel with pistols he had fought. He thought that the story applied to his life in some way as well. But associating himself with power and manliness didn't stave off his growing feelings of inadequacy.

That night, Kappler reportedly made love with Tommie. But she still couldn't tell how troubled he was. A failure to perform with her would probably have been devastating to him.

"Well, it's possible," Kappler would tell Dr. Kelso, "if you don't mind my suggesting what may or may not be true, the feelings of inadequacy that I was feeling in the previous days made me want to prove myself. I know it's perfectly bizarre for a man to want to prove himself by attempting to kill two people, but that's what I thought."

Kappler woke early on Saturday, April 14, to load the car for his solo drive back home to Los Angeles via New York. Their daughter's roommate, Alex, began mapping out very detailed directions to the highway because the Kapplers were wary of Boston drivers. "You know, the way you people drive, we weren't used to it," Tommie later testified in court.

Kappler's need to prove himself was increasing. He has said that he believed the Snickers bars in his car meant that Tommie, Elsie, and Alex were laughing at him. "Snick means Nick, which is the name of the devil," he told Dr. Ebert.

An elderly man, noticing the California plates on Kappler's car, stopped to chat. Kappler believed that the man had purposefully sought him out, especially when he cautioned Kappler not to fall asleep at the wheel on his long drive.

Kappler spoke briefly with the man, then went back inside for breakfast, a croissant, which he thought symbolized his inferiority— "A cross-ant. I was an ant and they were crossing me," he told Dr. Ebert—and coffee, served in a mug that Kappler has said was imprinted with the words, "You're damned if you do and you're damned if you don't.'' He thought Tommie "was telling me I have to do it. I didn't know what *it* is. I thought Tomy [*sic*] knows. She's giving me a tip. She's saying we have no alternative.''

Kappler left most of his food, told the group that he had better get going, and kissed Tommie good-bye. It was approximately 10:00 A.M.

"I remember going down the stairs thinking . . . that there was something horrendous that had to be done,'' he told Dr. Ebert. "A great challenge. That I had no alternative. I got in the car and I started.''

Asked whether he knew his victim, Kappler would respond, "My God, I don't know anybody in Boston. I didn't know he was a physician.''

# FIRST PERSON

> For the illness is not a superfluous and senseless burden, it is himself; he himself is that "other" . . .

> —Carl Jung

Paul Mendelsohn, like me, believed that life is not made up of random events; rather, meaningful connections link the earliest chapters of our lives with the most recent ones. He had refined the skills and, perhaps, been born with the intuitions to unmask frightening psychiatric symptoms, like psychosis, and find the hurt—the humanity—fueling them. He believed that lives, even those tending toward darkness, could be understood.

He had discovered that his work could not be done from a distance; the demons of the mind thrive in isolation and can be vanquished only by extending them a hand. To do this work often requires of psychiatrists that they find the weakest, most fearful, and even most frightening parts of patients in themselves. This kind of empathic witnessing has the power to heal people, in ways that cannot fully be explained.

According to his wife, Camille, Paul was fascinated with killers. He had read books about Charles Manson and Ted Bundy. "They represented so much of Paul's disowned stuff," she said. ". . . I think maybe Paul's deep psyche drew him to psychiatry. He never did anything crazy. He never did anything weird."

Could Paul Mendelsohn, a gentle man, have found

enough of John Kappler in himself to have helped him listen to his own terror instead of hearing voices? Could he have helped him look at his own suffering instead of recreating it in others?

Everything I know about Paul leads me to believe that he would have rejected the notion that Kappler's periods of paranoia and bizarre behavior were nothing more than manifestations of brain chemistry gone awry, sterile signs and symptoms of one or another disorder. He would not have been content to name Kappler's suffering without understanding it.

While insisting that Kappler take his medicines and meticulously monitoring their use, he would have gone on to wonder what life events had spawned Kappler's pathologic fear and behavior, what experiences had made the shared world of reality and morality an untenable one for him to live in. He would have taken Kappler's silence about Pittsburgh as a clue that unspeakable wrongs had been done him there.

The acknowledgment that harm had been done John Kappler, that he had suffered and been broken, might have provided the essential foundation on which to build an empathic relationship with him.

It would have been an enormously hard, perhaps impossible, alliance to forge, but I believe Paul would have understood that the difficulties encountered in connecting with a man like Kappler, including his dishonesty and manipulativeness, reflect the importance he had come to place on not being known and not being controlled by anyone.

If Paul felt repulsed, frustrated, or bored by Kappler, he would have had to search for the reasons he was feeling such emotions. Was his patient, he would have had to wonder, subtly trying to make him keep his distance?

A man like Kappler might become angriest, most detached, even sickest at those times his psychiatrist edges closest to the truths about his life. The rage and even the psychosis has to be seen for what it is: the flamethrower of a fortress under siege. Pleasantries, humor, and easy exchanges might be clues that no real work is being done.

There can be no retreat on the psychiatrist's part. One patient with a psychotic illness has written: "The doctor has to feel sure he has the right to break into the illness, just as a parent knows he has the right to walk into a baby's room, no matter what the baby feels about it. The doctor has to know he's [or she's] doing the right thing. . . . Some people go through life with vomit on their lips. You can feel their terrible hunger but they defy you to feed them."

Sitting with Kappler for long enough, there might be opportunities to break in: notable inconsistencies in his stories about his life, irrational and interpretable feelings toward the psychiatrist, slips of the tongue, periods of depression when the mask falls away. Paul would have had to take every opportunity to circle toward the truth, slowly unmasking the contradictions and self-hatred under Kappler's narcissism, the fear of intimacy that colored his family life, the self-doubt beneath his professional persona. By serving as the catalyst for Kappler to reveal his darkest dramas, yet without ever condemning him, Paul would be letting the light in.

Examining the darkness in Kappler would have required Paul to acknowledge and explore the darkness in himself. If a psychiatrist cannot look with equanimity at the injured and rageful parts of himself, he will balk at calling forth and embracing those of his patient.

I believe Paul Mendelsohn would have stood a small chance of doing some part of this not because he was a saint but because he was so exquisitely human. Not above the fray, he was open to hearing and feeling people's pain, willing for his soul to become the battleground for confrontations between health and illness, good and evil.

# PART FOUR

# JUSTICE

# CHAPTER 11

Psychiatry having failed to heal him, his colleagues having looked the other way, his wife having cast her own shadow over his life, the criminal justice system having failed to contain him, John Kappler had finally left behind undeniable evidence of his destructiveness.

Shortly after Paul Mendelsohn and Deborah Brunet-Tuttle were rushed to the Massachusetts General Hospital, Metropolitan Police officers Richard Karsh and Scott Wilson, experts in accident reconstruction, arrived at the scene of the crime. They noted that there were no skid marks or any other sign of braking between the two piles of debris where Kappler's victims had fallen. Nor was there any damage to the trees adjacent to the jogging path.

After a brief search, they found Kappler's 1989 Hyundai Sonata, its windshield broken and splattered with blood and half a blue plastic Easter egg jammed between the car's spoiler and radiator. Inside the car were clothing, Snickers bars, and bottles of medication, including the mood stabilizer lithium, an antidepressant called Doxepin, and an antipsychotic called thioridazine. Kappler's name appeared on the medication bottles as both patient and physician.

Using microfiche records from the California Registry of Motor Vehicles, Kappler was identified as the owner of the car. Police located his daughter Elsie in Medford. When the officers arrived at Elsie's apartment later, Tommie gave them an inaccurate description of Kappler's clothing. She also did not tell them that he had left a disturbing telephone message on Elsie's answering machine or that he had a history of violence and psychosis.

Kappler, by this time, was making his way out of the state by bus. His journey ended in New York City in the Payne Whitney Clinic, where Tommie flew to see him on April 16.

"He was hostile, and he was lying on the bed," she later testified, "and he didn't get up to even speak to me. And, he just—he didn't even seem glad to see me or anything. He just seemed, sort of, remote. You know, he was upset."

She brought him candy, but he wouldn't eat it, which led her to believe he was psychotic.

Kappler was treated with lithium and the tranquilizing medicine lorazepam during his five-day stay. He was noted to sleep well and to have a good appetite. According to hospital records, he showed no obvious signs of psychosis at any time. He did, however, pace a great deal and move his feet nervously. While being transferred from one unit to another, he grabbed a bunch of exposed electrical wires, later explaining, "I was hoping to electrocute myself."

He stayed in close touch with his attorney.

Marcy Jackson was the assistant district attorney assigned to the Kappler case. Still in her early thirties, it was one of her first murder cases.

With dark hair, bright blue eyes, and a dancer's build, Jackson was pretty enough that strangers didn't always expect the potent combination of her high intellect and razor-sharp humor, but in the district attorney's office, she was well known for fierce determination.

The daughter of a wealthy construction contractor, she had grown up in Newton, an affluent suburb of Boston, and graduated from Boston College School of Law. Before joining the district attorney's office, she had worked on Senator Ted Kennedy's presidential campaign and as an aide in his Washington, D.C., office.

Until long after Kappler's trial, Jackson, who had moved on to a special unit prosecuting Boston gang members, was unaware of the details of his upbringing. During an interview with me, she seemed surprised to learn that he had been born poor, to teenagers who abused him. "Well, that's interesting," she said after a few moments of reflection, "but it's also irrelevant to the case."

Jackson was also unable to relate any significant event in her own life to her choice of careers or to her passionate conviction that transgressors should be made to pay for their offenses.

A cynic at core, a prosecutor nearly by nature, she was primed to doubt that Kappler had merely followed the commands of voices when he threaded his way out of state by car, commuter rail, and bus. She would come to suspect, in fact, that he had not only knowingly fled after killing Mendelsohn but that he had fabricated his psychiatric symptoms for decades.

Jackson was also energized by the prospect of opposing Kappler's lawyer, Jonathan Shapiro. Shapiro, who wore a silver beard, was fifty years old and well into a career punctuated by highly publicized civil rights and murder cases. If his professorial tone with Jackson was designed to intimidate her, it failed.

After being assigned to Kappler's case and learning from Shapiro where the accused was, Jackson set about clearing the many legal and administrative hurdles necessary to bring Kappler back to face charges in Massachusetts. On April 18, her efforts bore fruit. Officer Scott Wilson and state trooper Joe Lawless flew to New York City and met with detectives at the Nineteenth Precinct police station. The next morning they visited the Payne Whitney Clinic together and placed Kappler under arrest. At a hearing later that day, he put forward no legal challenge to his being returned to Massachusetts.

As Wilson and Lawless were taking him to a waiting car for the ride to La Guardia airport, Kappler muttered, "You might as well just shoot me now."

Kappler was flown out on the last Trump shuttle to Boston. Tommie and attorney Shapiro were also passengers. After arriving at the Logan Airport State Police Barracks, he stated that he "loved" his car and that it handled "just fabulous."

Months later, Lawless summed up his impressions of Kappler in a few words. "The guy's a thrill seeker," he said.

The next day, Kappler was interviewed by Cambridge court clinic psychiatrist Prudence Baxter to assess whether he had the capacity to understand the court proceedings during which he would be charged. Baxter later wrote, in part:

> While on the advice of his attorney Dr. Kappler did not discuss the incident that led to his arrest he did say that he had not been taking his lithium for some months until several days before the incident. He said he resumed taking it because of "sign posts I follow frequently that can be mysteriously wrong. Sometimes I get an insecure feeling. It frightens me. It may be that I'll see a piece of a delusion and it

prompts sufficient fear that I might have a whole delusion." He said that he had one of these "insecure feelings" several days before the incident and started taking the medication again. He said that he started hearing voices the morning of the incident. His attorney instructed him not to discuss the content of the voices. He also said that he has most recently experienced one of his delusional experiences the day of the alleged incident.

Baxter found no defect in the way Kappler organized his thoughts and noted that he denied that the voices were still with him. He did, however, claim that he still thought some seemingly casual incidents harbored messages for him. On seeing the word "funeral" on a sign, for instance, he initially "thought the message was for him and spoke to what would happen to him."

He reported thinking about suicide because it would avert the terribly difficult painful road ahead for him and his family. "He spoke of his 'cowardice' in terms of hurting himself," Baxter wrote, "but said 'if someone stuck a gun in my ear' that would be OK. . . ."

Baxter wrote that while Kappler was polite, cooperative and composed during his evaluation by her, he became visibly anxious and agitated and "appeared tearful" in the courtroom when the charges against him were read.

Kappler was found competent to participate in the court proceedings. He was charged with murder in the second degree, armed assault with intent to murder, and assault and battery with a dangerous weapon (a motor vehicle).

Officer Wilson served Kappler with a warrant to confiscate his clothing as evidence and offered to provide him with clothing from the Sheriff's Department.

"Are you just harassing me?" Kappler reportedly asked.

# CHAPTER 12

After being charged, Kappler was deemed a continued suicide risk and transferred to Metropolitan State Hospital to await trial and begin a battery of psychiatric evaluations.

The role of psychiatry had now changed. When Kappler was a free man, its primary function was to heal him. Now it was used to supply data that could help jurors judge him.

Kappler's plea of not guilty by reason of insanity would have to satisfy the M'Naughten rule, first used in Great Britain in 1843: "To establish a defense on the ground of insanity, it must be clearly proved that, at the time of the committing of the act, the party accused was labouring under such a defect of reason, from disease of the mind, as not to know the nature and quality of the act he was doing; or if he did know it, that he did not know he was doing what was wrong."

In everyday language, the rule means that anyone invoking the insanity defense must meet two criteria to be found innocent: (1) he or she was suffering from a major mental illness at the time of the crime, and (2) the major mental illness either made it impossible for the person to

Kappler (*far right*) attends the prom at the Taylor Allderdice High School, located on the corner of Shady and Forward Avenues in Pittsburgh. The school was outside Kappler's neighborhood and filled with students more affluent than himself.

A graduation picture from Taylor Allderdice. Kappler would go on to the University of Pittsburgh, a stint in the Army, and then Emory University before attending medical school.

Kappler with a favorite aunt in a New York City restaurant.
Despite episodes of drunkenness and disobedience, Kappler
was awarded the Army's meritorious bronze star.

Kappler in uniform during the Korean War. He worked as a teletype operator and saw close combat only once.

Two portraits of the Kapplers with their first child, a girl. The infant died of cancer while John Kappler was completing his second year of medical school at Bowman Gray School of Medicine, a year he later called "hell."

Kappler during his anesthesiology residency. He had already been hospitalized for psychosis.

Two photos of John and Tommie Kappler in later years. He once called his marriage "the most significant event" in his life.

John F. Kappler listens to the judge presiding over his 1985 arraignment on charges of attempted murder for disconnecting a patient's respirator. As always, his wife Tommie (in profile) was by his side.

**Los Angeles Times**

Tuesday, May 14, 1985

## Doctor Accused of Cutting Off Patient's Life Support System

By PAUL FELDMAN,
*Times Staff Writer*

A Van Nuys physician was charged with attempted murder on Monday for allegedly
~~...~~ ~~...~~ ~~...~~orization, the life
~~...~~

**Los Angeles Times**

Wednesday, June 12, 1985

## Doctor Freed of Attempted Murder Count

By PAUL FELDMAN, *Times Staff Writer*

A charge of attempted murder was dismissed Tuesday against Dr. John Frederick Kappler, a Van Nuys physician whom authorities had accused of removing, without authorization, the life-support system of a brain-damaged patient at Hollywood Presbyterian Medical Center last Apr.

Los Angeles Municipal Judge Edward L. Davenport dismissed the charge after a two-day preliminary ~~...~~ which prosecutors were unable to provide ~~...~~uld positively ~~...~~ hospital ~~...~~ ~~...~~cal

With no one able to testify to seeing Kappler disconnect Ben Wytewa's respirator, the charges against him were dismissed. "The mere fact that the charge was levied," Kappler complained, "[means] that if anything happens in a hospital and I don't have an alibi, I'm screwed."

Kappler's 1989 Hyundai Sonata, its hood dented and wind-shield broken by the impact of his victims' bodies. He had made sure to aim the right side of the car at Dr. Paul Mendelsohn "...If I'd have hit him on the left," he later said, "he might have come through the windshield on my side....I certainly wouldn't have been able to continue on for the second one."

tell right from wrong or made it impossible for him or her to comply with the law.

With rare exceptions, courts do not recognize disorders of character, no matter how severe, as constituting a mental disease. The jails are full of people, for example, with psychopathic (antisocial) personality disorder.

From the start, Kappler's evaluation seemed to raise as many questions as it answered. Dr. Christie Emigh, the admitting physician at Metropolitan State Hospital, noted that while Kappler was generally organized and coherent, he intermittently became tearful and agitated and grimaced dramatically. But she wasn't convinced his emotional instability reflected any underlying psychosis. She wrote, in fact, that Kappler showed no evidence of hearing voices or seeing visions.

Kappler told her that for two months prior to his journey east, he had slept only four hours a night and his appetite and level of energy had fallen off during the trip. People with mania, however, typically experience *increased* energy.

He further confided that while traveling to New York City after killing Paul Mendelsohn, he believed the police were after him, wanted to arrest him, and might even shoot him—thoughts that suggest he may have known he had done something unlawful. Yet he would later report that far from fearing the police, he had taken their sirens at the crime scene as a form of congratulations.

Dr. Emigh thought Kappler might be suffering from mania, atypical psychosis, or both. With her assessment, the number of different conditions psychiatrists at one time or another believed Kappler might suffer from rose to four: major depression, paranoid schizophrenia, mania (the "high" phase of bipolar disorder), and, now, atypical psychosis.

Atypical psychosis is a diagnosis created by the American Psychiatric Association (APA) to cover patients who say they suffer with delusions or hallucinations but do not evidence the usual symptoms of better-known psychotic illnesses, like schizophrenia. This diagnosis, however, is just a label. There is no evidence that people with atypical psychosis have specific brain abnormalities in common or have suffered through similar life experiences. There is no reason to believe they will be helped by the same treatment.

Psychiatrists sometimes call diagnoses like atypical psychosis "garbage pail" diagnoses, because they don't know what afflicts the patients who fall in these categories. They are testimony to the fact that the medical model of sorting patients by diagnosis has been stretched beyond reason to cover the pathology in psychiatry's domain. Increasingly, labeling patients is passing for understanding them. And to the extent that the charade diverts attention from ferreting out the underlying psychological issues fueling symptoms, men like John Kappler can slip through the health care system untouched and unchanged.

The confusion is multiplied when psychiatrists testify in court. If they don't have confidence in their own diagnostic framework, is it any surprise that lawyers and judges are sometimes baffled by it?

Kappler was transferred to the Taunton State Hospital on April 23 for a psychological evaluation specifically designed to assess his level of criminal responsibility for his actions. Forensic psychologist J. Tyler Carpenter, who interviewed him at length, wrote in his report that while Kappler expressed discomfort with having an unpolished, " 'plebeian' " background, his personal style was actually "quite polished if not a little too much so." Carpenter thought his patient was being excessively deferential toward him.

Contrary to the picture Kappler would later paint of symptoms building over the course of several days of travel, he told Carpenter that his mood remained stable as he traveled from Los Angeles to Boston and that he was under no stress the morning he struck Paul Mendelsohn and Deborah Brunet-Tuttle. Although he had previously stated that more than one voice had directed him to drive off the road and journey to New York, he now told Carpenter a single voice had guided him throughout. He became very anxious when confronted with the disparity.

Carpenter's report states:

> At the close of the evaluation, this examiner asked him about the inconsistencies in the record and in his narration concerning the number of voices. Dr. Kappler became quite pale and shaken and said that maybe he had been remembering a prior episode, years before, when he had in fact heard several voices. He again insisted that he had heard only one voice on the day in question and was not in any emotional distress on that day. In fact, he said, it could have been his own voice talking to himself on that day.

Kappler took a number of psychological tests, including the Minnesota Multiphasic Personality Inventory (MMPI), Thematic Appercepton Test (TAT), and Rorschach, designed to assess his personality traits and identify his underlying thought patterns. Carpenter wrote in his report that the tests showed a "striking" absence of signs suggesting current psychosis and a lack of significant signs of suicidality. The personality profile showed Kappler as "introverted, self-conscious and passive-dependent" and the type of person who might have feelings of "inadequacy and self-dissatisfaction beneath a facade of competence and calm." He seemed embarrassed by his modest—"plebeian"—social background and average performance in medical school.

The testing revealed other conflicts, as well. While Kappler told Carpenter he was satisfied with his life and happy to be rid of his childhood environment, some data suggested "themes of deeper, perhaps less conscious, alienation, frustration, and unhappiness at being estranged from one's roots."

Carpenter's report went on to suggest that Kappler's test scores were of a variety commonly found among prisoners:

> . . . He endorsed a notable number of items on several scales suggesting that he may enjoy the exploits of criminals, as well as feel justified in harboring misanthropic attitudes. It is possible that lawlessness provides him with a vicarious enjoyment that he doesn't get from his more conventional adjustment and that it perhaps satisfies some repressed need that has its origins in his reportedly chaotic childhood. He endorsed a significant number of items suggesting that he is uncomfortable and unhappy with himself, doesn't find daily living rewarding (not certain to what degree this is a by-product of his incarceration), and may feel vague guilt and remorse for past deeds (Dr. Kappler endorsed an item which said he has made lots of bad mistakes in his life. He should be interviewed as to exactly what he meant when he answered this question affirmatively). People with this code often tend to act out again in spite of their resolutions. People with his borderline moderate to high Pd elevation [a statistical measure of person-

ality] may be described as impulsive, adventurous, resentful, impatient, and imaginative.

. . . Dr. Kappler's predominant affects are moderate depression and anxiety, most likely related to the consequences following his alleged acts. He makes extensive use of repression and seems to have difficulty managing anger and aggression. He received a high score on the Over-controlled Hostility Scale suggesting that he is someone who tends to respond to provocation appropriately most of the time, but occasionally displays exaggerated aggressive responses without provocation. He received a low score on the Dominance scale suggesting a dynamic in which his usual interpersonal posture is submissive and unassertive rather than appropriately assertive. He also received a low score on a scale measuring anger, suggesting that he does not see himself as having the same amount of this emotion as many people do.

Carpenter put forward six possible diagnoses of Kappler's condition bringing his number of lifetime diagnoses to at least ten, among them atypical bipolar disorder, in remission; organic mental disorder, in remission; brief reactive psychosis, in remission; adjustment disorder and mixed personality disorder with passive-dependent and antisocial features. The first diagnosis on Carpenter's list, however, was malingering, the deliberate simulation or exaggeration of an illness or disability to avoid an unpleasant situation or to obtain some type of personal gain. In other words, Carpenter wondered whether Kappler might be fabricating his symptoms to avoid prison.

\*   \*   \*

The possibility that Kappler was faking some or all of his symptoms seemed to gather weight during his stay at Taunton State. Douglas McMurtry, one of the social workers treating him there, met with him on May 15 to assess how his visit with his son, Jack, had gone the previous evening.

According to the medical record, Kappler opened the meeting by stating that he felt sexually frustrated and wanted to perform oral sex on McMurtry. When McMurtry declined and explained the proper boundaries between clinicians and patients, Kappler seemed to urge McMurtry to record his proposition as evidence of mental illness.

"He did state," McMurtry wrote in the record, "that, in documenting our interaction, if I thought that his behavior was at all bizarre, I should note that he has been periodically psychotic on the unit and, in fact, throughout the course of his life. He stated that he hoped I would keep this in mind and that I might think that, perhaps, his state of mind in speaking with me could have been similar to his state of mind at the time of the 'court issues.' "

The state's case against Kappler was also strengthened by a meticulous assessment of him performed at Taunton State by forensic psychologist Frederick Kelso. Kelso met separately with Kappler and Tommie for several hours, spoke by telephone with Elsie and Jack, and reviewed all the available medical records on Kappler back to his hospitalizations in the 1960s. He came up with three different ways to understand Kappler's destructiveness and level of responsibility for it. Each seemed at least plausible to him.

In Model A, Kelso gave Kappler the benefit of the doubt by assuming that the psychiatric symptoms he reported, including the voices that told him to hit Paul Mendelsohn and Deborah Brunet-Tuttle, were real. Supporting this hypothesis was the fact that Kappler had been hospitalized many times in the past and that numerous clinicians had diagnosed him with one or another serious mental disorder.

But there were difficulties with accepting Model A, according to Kelso, including the unusual nature of the signs and symptoms of Kappler's presumed disorder. Unlike most other psychiatric conditions, Kappler's seemed to disappear for years, surface for hours or days, then disappear again. More than once his symptoms responded very quickly to antipsychotic medications, which typically take much longer to work.

Kelso was also troubled by the fact that Kappler's psychological testing by J. Tyler Carpenter had revealed no underlying psychosis and that, despite Kappler's sense that a voice or voices had been with him even as a child, there was no information from his youth that seemed to confirm it.

The voices themselves were unusual, in Kelso's view. Whereas psychotic individuals typically report hearing voices through their ears, much like hearing any other speech, Kappler consistently reported that the voices originated inside his head and were continuous over periods of many hours. Psychotic patients, in contrast, often report more intermittent hallucinations. Finally, Kelso noted that Kappler himself had expressed the possibility that the voices "could have been his own voice talking to him."

Even granting that Kappler heard voices and was mentally ill, Kelso still struggled in Model A with whether his patient could have refused to do what the voices said. Was he driven to his act of destruction, or did he decide to commit it?

A key issue here is the extent to which the defendant could do nothing other than "obey" the directives of his auditory hallucinations, contrasted with his ability to consider, and take, courses of action somewhat independently of the directives of his hallucinations. The defendant provided me consequences of the hit and run, or that it would be taken care of in some way. At one point, John Kappler told me "I don't go through any thought process—I just do what it [the "voice"] says."

But Kelso said there was reason to believe Kappler did think before he acted violently. He highlighted Kappler's statements about "consciously deciding . . . to hit him [the male jogger] on the right," having "calculated a path [in which to drive the car]," and having "a feeling of determination" as consistent with the idea that Kappler made thoughtful choices at the time of his assaultiveness. Similarly, Kelso noted Kappler had spoken of consciously evaluating the messages he said he was receiving:

There is also the problem of the extent to which the defendant was actively *interpreting* the communications he says he was receiving from his voices. Examples of this would be when the defendant told me "by this time, I might have been extending what I was hearing," and at another point, when he told me "I can't recall if the voice or voices were giving me confusing instructions, or if I'd hear the seed of an idea and enlarge upon it myself," and when he told me "every once in a while there would be a stronger suggestion which would keep me on the path I eventually chose."

Model A thus would leave the jury plenty of room to question whether Kappler's symptoms met the conditions for innocence in the M'Naughten rule. Model B, in contrast, seemed to justify any suspicion they might ulti-mately harbor that he was simply fabricating his symptoms. The premise of this model was that Kappler was unintentionally or intentionally distorting his report of what he experienced the day of the crime.

One possible form of distortion that Kelso raised was relatively benign. Perhaps, he theorized, Kappler's sincere struggle to recall some details about the voice (or voices) he heard and to make sense of the tragedy for himself might have led him unwittingly to alter his recollections of what he experienced that day. He wrote:

> A kind of picture develops in which the defendant might perhaps have afterwards thought to himself something like "I must have been psychotic to do something like that—I wouldn't have done that un-less the voice had so instructed me."

But Model B also encompassed that darkest of possi-bilities: Kappler might be malingering, consciously fab-ricating or embellishing symptoms to affect the outcome of his case. There was, after all, the record of Kappler's having become pale and shaken when confronted by Dr. Carpenter with the discrepancy in his reports of being directed by one voice versus several voices. There was the matter of Kappler's insisting he was powerless to re-sist the voices but in fact resisting them when they called for him to harm himself.

There was also a difference in two of Kappler's reports of when the voice first took control of him on April 14. He told Carpenter the voice visited him only upon enter-ing his car to begin the long trip home. But he reportedly told Kelso that it had begun speaking to him in Elsie's apartment.

"Another factor," Kelso wrote, "is the issue of the

defendant more than once *calling attention to his symptoms*." He cited Kappler's suggestion to Douglas McMurtry that he interpret his bizarre sexual advance as a reflection of mental illness. When Kelso brought up the McMurtry episode during a meeting with Kappler, in fact, Kappler told him he hadn't lost interest. He offered to perform oral sex on Kelso himself, who, of course, refused. "My classification here suggests that if you report this to the court—that it probably won't hurt my case," Kappler told him at the time. "That's obviously of concern to me."

Perhaps most damaging to Kappler was his apparent plan to dupe the court. "It's going to be very difficult in the courtroom," he told Kelso. "They always desire remorse, it will be kind of hard to manufacture."

Kelso had a third model, Model C, in which Kappler was seen as psychologically impaired when he killed Paul Mendelsohn but not primarily by a major mental illness like bipolar disorder, atypical psychosis, or schizophrenia. His "symptoms" and acts, the model suggested, were due instead to a disorder of personality extremely deep, nearly lifelong flaws in his character. It was this model that came closest to labeling Kappler a psychopath. Kelso cited Kappler's narcissism and antisocial behavior back to his teens. He theorized that the trip east may indeed have eroded Kappler's fragile self-esteem, laying bare the intolerable feelings of weakness and helplessness that lurked just below the surface, legacies of childhood abuse left unexamined to boil, and then boil over. Destructiveness was his way of regaining his vision of himself as manly, capable, and formidable:

In this model of the defendant's mental condition at the time of the events in question, the defendant would not be seen as experiencing auditory hallucinations in the typical sense. Rather, the defendant's experience of hearing a voice inside his head would be understood as, quite literally, the defendant "talking to himself."

... The defendant's behavior at the time of the events in question is thus understood as his attempt to cope with the feelings of inadequacy, deficiency, and failure he was experiencing, doing so in a way that reestablished, in his own mind, his masculine sense of control and mastery and importance over his life.

# CHAPTER 13

On June 22, Kappler was transferred from Taunton State Hospital to the prestigious McLean Hospital in Belmont, Massachusetts. His attending psychiatrist was Dr. Robert Aranow.

Documents from Kappler's stay at McLean suggest that he had at least partially rebuilt the armor of his false self. For one thing, his memories of his mental state when he ran down Paul Mendelsohn and Deborah Brunet-Tuttle were much clearer and generally more exonerating of himself.

He told John Lepore, a Harvard Medical School student working at the hospital, that he was certain a single, male voice with a computer-like tone and "overwhelming power" had issued the commands he followed. He also implied that his previous evaluations at Taunton State might be unreliable because they had been conducted while he was tormented by delusions that devils were in control there and were killing his children one by one. He noted that he commonly concealed his symptoms because voices commanded him to do so. The psychosis, he said, lasted a little over a week into his admission to McLean, then suddenly lifted like a fog.

"He could tell the rank of devil of each person based on the color of their clothes," Lepore wrote in his case report, and his placement on the red team [treatment group] as opposed to the blue team signified that he was designated to suffer in this hell."

Lepore recorded Kappler's major concerns as the risk of medication side effects, the disgrace he had visited upon himself and his family, and his upcoming trial. "Concerning these latter two points," he wrote, "it is generally agreed among those who have spoken with him that he feels a terrible sense of guilt for what he has and will put his family through, but that it is less readily apparent that he has similar feelings concerning the victims of the hit and run. He did, however, appear to shed tears during rounds when this matter was discussed.

". . . It is not apparent that he is fully aware that he actually caused the death of a man or that he feels remorse for this act or sympathy for the family."

Kappler was already fashioning a storybook role for himself should he be found guilty at trial and imprisoned. "He appears unfrightened of a jail sentence," Lepore wrote, "stating that many people before him have survived jail without great trouble and that perhaps he'll play a role of 'the Doc Watson' whom the other inmates will come to for medical advice."

Lepore and others at McLean noted Kappler's near-obsession with neatness and order. He meticulously made his bed each morning, smoothing the sheets and arranging the pillows painstakingly; spent much of his free time cleaning the ward kitchen and sitting room; and picked lint from the clothing of clinicians he met with.

Further psychological testing, however, continued to reveal that Kappler's bravado and orderliness were flimsy masks over deeper feelings of weakness and rage. A report on testing by McLean's John Foehl noted that Kappler's respectful tone, sophisticated vocabulary, and expressions of a desire to be helpful during the interview seemed like a defense:

> There were times . . . when this professorial ease seemed to be forced, to be unreflectively used as a means of smoothing over less appealing thoughts and feelings. Dr. Kappler grimaced with his hand to his forehead at one point in the testing, leading me to ask how he was feeling.

> "Don't worry, I won't hurt you," he responded with a wry smile, reaching over and picking a small piece of lint from my pant leg. His seemingly avuncular playfulness did not mask the anger and intrusiveness of his gesture.

Foehl believed, in fact, that Kappler had probably struggled throughout his life to cover up his real feelings of depression, self-hatred, and fear:

> In spite of rising to the status of M.D., and superficially presenting himself in a manner which well fits this status it is likely that he has felt this to be a sham, that, given his humble origins, he has in fact risen well above what he would consider his rightful place.

Acting ragefully, Foehl wrote, had been Kappler's way of escaping his chronic, painful feelings:

> . . . Although he has attempted to put on a good, happy appearance, it has been extremely difficult to maintain. This has led to a more primitive dissociation and projective defenses as a means of dealing

with his painful sense of guilt, loneliness and humiliation.

Dr. Kappler has been successful in animating himself away from depressive affect, however, through his tendency to be unreflectively rageful. He has been extremely angry both as a response to his experienced desolation and loneliness, and as a counterphobic means of counteracting his extreme discomfort with feeling effeminate, weak, powerless and despondent.

In direct opposition to Tyler Carpenter's psychological examination of Kappler, Foehl's report asserted that psychosis might still lurk beneath Kappler's armor. Kappler's answers to specific questions from Foehl were fairly commonplace, but when invited to elaborate freely, his responses revealed an "exceedingly idiosyncratic, autistic and bizarre world of thoughts and experiences" which Foehl believed were psychotic in nature. When asked to comment on a Rorschach ink blot, for instance, Kappler initially remarked that it resembled a space ship. Then, however, he continued that " '. . . it's a comic book space ship because they often look like flying bats or birds or other animals. Serious adult ships are involved with ion drive, accommodating many people. Children's space ships show a person riding on the back of it with reins.' "

Foehl emphasized that Kappler's mask of sanity was usually a convincing one:

. . . This man's propensity for psychotic thinking and experience is extremely deceptive and subtle. In spite of clear psychotic content, Dr Kappler's adroit manner of responding made it extremely difficult to acknowledge the significance of his bizarre responses as manifestations of psychotic thinking. Peculiar content was often accompanied by a chuckle, or a knowing grin, which tended to disarmingly distract us both from his at times highly peculiar and frightening images. One might easily make sense of his narcissistic posturing, his unaffected social sophistication, as an indication of antisocial characterological traits. But as seen through the testing, this stance is more appropriately understood as an unreflectively defensive paranoid attitude through which he dissociates, minimizes, denies and projects bizarre, aggressive and depressive aspects of his experience.

Foehl concluded that Kappler's psychological equilibrium was fragile and could topple, particularly in the setting of challenges to his narcissism, "into a rather bizarre and frighteningly autistic world of threatening images" in which his self-hatred was projected outward:

Although Dr. Kappler is clearly not actively and floridly psychotic at this time, his predisposition for psychotic experiences makes it likely that at times of decreased structure and increased stress this predisposition may break through to an overt decompensation. It is quite within reason to expect that he would experience paranoid delusions, auditory and visual hallucinations.

... At such times, he is highly likely to impulsively act on his violent urges, directing his actions toward himself or toward nameless others. He must be seen as at extreme risk for self harm and for potentially harming others.

Dr. Robert Aranow believed that Kappler experienced genuine and severe psychosis as well. He theorized he suffered with *psychotic disorder not otherwise specified* (a different name for *atypical psychosis*) and was probably much sicker most of the time than he let on. In a July 13, 1990, progress note he wrote:

> A recently available evaluation from Taunton State suggest [sic] the possibility of a diagnosis of malingering or brief reactive psychosis. It is hard to imagine how the symptomatology described in this chart with the extraordinary degrees of impulsive, unplanned, and devastatingly self-incriminating and destructive behaviors could warrant this diagnosis. As noted, on 7/10/90 in this chart, Dr. Kappler's clinical descriptions have progressively indicated the presence of psychotic thinking and behavior for larger and larger amounts of his past. Clinical data also indicates that neuroleptics [antipsychotic medications] have been effective in reducing his symptomatology during the acute episodes. Unfortunnately, it does not appear that Dr. Kappler has been maintained on standing [ongoing] neuroleptics for prolonged periods which might be warranted in view of the extraordinary risks created by his psychosis.

But even Aranow's note, as insistent as it was that Kappler wasn't faking, veered off into questions about his character. "Up to the present," he wrote, "Dr. Kappler has demonstrated notably limited interest in any treatments that might help to prevent what he describes as terrifying and have been obviously harmful episodes."

Aranow offered Kappler the option of taking the new and highly effective antipsychotic medication Clozaril, but Kappler rejected the idea because the medicine carries a very small risk of fatal bone marrow suppression. None of the available notes from Aranow explain how Kappler could be so worried about avoiding injury from medication at the same time as he was telling staff at McLean that he was contemplating suicide.

The question of whether Kappler's behavior was primarily due to a major mental illness like bipolar disorder (manic-depressive disorder) or to a psychopathic personality would be of critical importance during his trial. With rare exceptions, psychopaths, no matter how extraordinary their thoughts and behaviors, do not meet the criteria for innocence by reason of insanity. The presumption is that they are bad and deserving of punishment.

The official diagnostic manual of psychiatry lists psychopathic (antisocial) personality as a disorder, but having drifted from its roots in morality and ethics, the field has lost much of its calling and its authority to elucidate the philosophical issues of personal responsibility, evil, and illness that labeling people with such a "disorder" raises.

In the eyes of the judicial system, the core distinction between psychopaths and patients with a major mental illness is whether the condition can rob them of free will. Psychopaths are presumed to act by choice against others; manic or schizophrenic patients commanded by voices to kill are sometimes seen as "taken over" by renegade chemical messengers in the brain.

This is one reason that clinicians spent so much time and energy highlighting the inconsistencies in Kappler's recollections, noting the unusual nature of his symptoms and documenting his requests that his bizarre behavior be recorded for the court. They were establishing the possibility that Kappler might well be a manipulative liar—a psychopath—who, knowing murder was illegal, chose to kill Paul Mendelsohn because it made him feel powerful and then invented a cover story that included hearing voices.

But what is free will? Is it truly by choice that a man could find himself so fragile in his self-esteem that only trying to kill again and again could buoy it? Is it an act of free will to be disconnected from the suffering of others, empathically anesthetized, cut loose from the interpersonal ties that define humanity? Are there lives that tend, nearly unavoidably, toward darkness? And if so, do we call such people sick, or depraved, or both?

If John Foehl and Robert Aranow were wrong, if the presumed voices Kappler heard really were his own thoughts, if it mattered not a stitch whether there was one voice or two, if he knew that what he was doing was criminal and morally reprehensible but did it anyway, is he then a pure monster or part victim?

Paul Mendelsohn would have asked the question himself: What virulent brand of destruction must visit a man to lead him to destroy others?

# CHAPTER 14

I ask you for this man's head and I do so with a heart at
ease. . . . Never as strongly as today have I felt this painful
duty made easier, lighter, clearer by the certain knowledge
of a sacred imperative and by the horror I feel when I look
into a man's face and all I see is a monster.

—Albert Camus, *The Stranger*

John F. Kappler's trial began in the Cambridge Superior
Court on December 6, 1990, before Judge Robert "Buzz"
Barton, a measured man who at sixty still looked as if he
would make a fair linebacker, and had been a football and
baseball star at Dartmouth College. Partly in deference to
his father's wishes, he had turned down a career as a
professional baseball player to attend the Boston University Law School. "He was a very moral, very strict man,"
Barton said of his father, a city physician in Everett, Massachusetts, during the Depression. "He had a work ethic
that physicians don't have today."

Whether the law originally spoke to him or not, Buzz
Barton graduated number one in his class. He spent the
next three years as a lawyer in the Marines, defending
those facing general courts-martial. He met his wife after
a tour of duty in the Far East, while he was based in
California.

Barton left military service in 1959 and became an assistant district attorney in Massachusetts. He came to en-
joy the adversarial process because it reminded him of
athletic competition. Fueled by anger at doctors who

abused the privileges of their profession, he spent the next three years as the state's chief prosecutor of doctors accused of performing illegal abortions.

"My father told me these guys were butchers, and I believed him," Barton said. "Often, they were doctors who'd gotten into trouble in one way or another and didn't have any other way of making money. I do believe that because of my father and my relationship with him, I think anyone who disgraces medicine is disgracing my father's image and the way he practiced medicine."

After his years as an assistant district attorney, Barton entered the private practice of law in association with famed criminal defense attorney F. Lee Bailey. He was appointed to the bench in 1978.

Barton had a reputation of being fair but tough in administering the law as written. He harbored particularly strong misgivings about the insanity defense. He didn't think it should exist at all. "I personally don't feel that 'insanity' can excuse a person's debt to society on the most serious crimes we have," he told me.

Instead of a not-guilty-by-reason-of-insanity verdict, Barton felt juries should be given the option of finding defendants guilty but insane. "As long as they have a serious mental problem they'd be incarcerated in a place they get help," he explained, "then serve the rest of your sentence in a penal institution."

The idea that a verdict of guilty but insane should be created—a kind of umbrella under which psychiatrically ill offenders would be treated and then punished—might be greeted with disdain by many psychiatrists. The belief that the inherent goodness of some people can be overwhelmed by illnesses entirely foreign to them has been the raison d'etre for psychiatry's influence on the judicial system. Nevertheless, psychiatrists have sat rather silently for guilty verdicts on countless individuals who show clear and severe disorders of character. And they have remained silent even when such individuals are sentenced to death and executed.

Barton's instinct to hold all psychiatric patients accountable for their conduct—to lump them together rather than split them into moral categories—may actually be closer to central lines of reasoning within the field of psychiatry than initially seems to be the case. The truth is that many psychiatrists do not depersonalize major mental illness but rather see it as a reflection, albeit terribly distorted, of a patient's core emotions. In this sense mental illness is true *mad*ness. A large segment of the field, for example, would agree that rage that a patient cannot accept as a part of himself can be severed from consciousness and transformed into threatening voices. Paranoia can be a mirror image of a person's internal desire to harm others. Mania is sometimes understood as a flight from unbearable emotional suffering. If these symptoms of major mental illness are borne of core feelings, can they truly excuse individuals who kill while sick with them? Is anyone ever really "out of his mind"?

A patient I had treated for schizophrenia had been found not guilty by reason of insanity after killing his mother. She had made him sleep outside the house for several nights because she suspected him of using drugs. When he began hearing voices that told him she wasn't his mother at all but a clever imposter, they made sense to him. His real mother, he reasoned, would never have been so unfair.

Were the voices inexplicable by-products of an overabundant brain chemical or an expression of this patient's anger—a complete and chilling disavowal of the woman who had given birth to him? How should it weigh on his guilt or innocence that his anger might have contributed to his delusion? Was the illness, after all, wholly separate from him? And why is it that a disorder that mutates one's very character should inspire less pity and less immunity to punishment?

Another patient I treated was a teenager who had been raised in poverty by a cold and withholding mother and an extremely violent stepfather. He was small and asthmatic and an easy target for cruelty, not only of his parents but of other children. By age eight he had been identified as a behavioral problem in school and was diagnosed with a conduct disorder by a local psychiatrist. At ten he began to use marijuana and to steal. He was often truant. As he emerged into his teenage years, he became increasingly assaultive and was an ex-convict by the time he came to see me. He had lost an eye in a street fight. There was one short, thick scar on his upper arm from a knife injury. Another, slightly longer, zigzagged down his forearm. As if to warn me he could defend himself, he showed me his own switchblade.

"What things in life are you afraid of?" I asked him.

He stiffened and looked at me fiercely. "I'm not afraid of nothing," he bristled. "I can get hit, kicked, burned, knifed and I don't feel a thing. See, that's what's fucked about me. I have no fear. I don't feel pain." He shook his head. "And another thing, I get off seeing people bleed. Just the way someone's skin can split open, and the blood starts oozing. . . ." He leaned forward in his chair, genuinely excited, then rammed his fist into an open palm and settled back. "Now that ain't normal. To get all worked up over blood. That's fucked up, and I know it, but I can't stop it."

"Who stole it from you, do you think?" I asked.

"Stole what?" he sputtered. "Nobody takes anything from me and gets away with it."

"Your fear," I said gently. "Someone took all your

fear away. They've left you only with rage. See, you've been set up."

He sat quietly for several seconds, then reached into his pocket. I worried about the knife. "Being beat by my parents was bad," he said, "but there was other stuff—like this." He opened his wallet and handed me a wad of folded comic strips, given to him as a boy by his parents. In each, his parents had labeled the most idiotic character with his name.

With my patient's making a gift of those comic strips to me, we could begin to unearth the story of his violent life in earnest. It became increasingly clear to me how this slight, sickly, beaten, embarrassed, demeaned boy had grown into an angry and violent teenager. He already qualified for a diagnosis of antisocial (psychopathic) personality disorder.

If he were to kill years later, would it be fair to interpret that dark chapter in his life as entirely within his control? Or should he be considered hostage to an inescapable life story, in which the first chapters—written without his consent—had rooted the plot so deeply in pain and its disavowal that the final chapters, marked by impulsivity and destructiveness, had become nearly unavoidable? Would it be fair to equate the core of this young man any more completely with his disorder than in the case of the man who killed his mother?

Judge Barton's call for the creation of a guilty-but-insane verdict raises questions that psychiatry has forsaken. As we have tried to refine a medical model of mental illness, shaky at its base, throwing in our lot with the brain and denigrating the mind, we seem to be losing interest in the nature of human beings, the nature of suffering, and, indeed, the nature of guilt and innocence.

The judge's specific feelings about Kappler would be critical because by law he would have the power to set aside the jury's verdict should he feel it unsupported by the evidence presented in court.

His opinion of psychiatrists was pretty clear. "I've met a few I think are normal," he grinned.

# CHAPTER 15

Marcy Jackson delivered her opening statement to the jury first on December 6. She was dramatic and direct.

Tyler Carpenter, who had evaluated Kappler at Taunton State Hospital, had met with Jackson for several hours prior to the trial beginning. Although he had raised the possibility of Kappler's lying about his symptoms, he was nevertheless troubled by how readily Jackson embraced that possibility as a complete portrait of the man.

"I liked her," Carpenter told me. "I liked her energy and precision and zeal and her command of detail, but I had a hard time with her moral slant on it. I got the feeling that [she felt] what you saw was what you got. That he [Kappler] was bad and that he was lying to cover things up."

In fact, there was no question in Jackson's mind that Kappler was a criminal trying to get away with murder. Her moral outrage was obvious as she spoke to the jury.

"April 14, 1990, a Saturday, was a beautiful, bright spring day," Jackson began. "It was a spring day that was filled with new life, and it was a spring day, ladies and gentlemen, that also held death and destruction.

"The signs of life, ladies and gentlemen, were as a

result of acts of nature. The death and destruction, ladies and gentlemen, were as a result of the intentional, the deliberate, the conscious act of the Defendant, John Kappler.

"The Commonwealth will prove to you, ladies and gentlemen, that as a result of the intentional acts of John Kappler on April 14, 1990, a young man's life was brutally ended, and a young woman's life was forever damaged.

"The Commonwealth will prove to you beyond a reasonable doubt, that on April 14, 1990, at approximately 10:15 in the morning, the Defendant, John Kappler chose to drive his car, a car that he owned, a car that he was licensed to drive—chose to drive that car on the running path, the jogging path located between Henderson Street and Massachusetts Avenue, on the Cambridge/Somerville line.

"And, he drove that car onto that running path, ladies and gentlemen, on that bright spring day, at 10:15 in the morning. And he drove it on that path at approximately thirty to forty miles per hour.

"The evidence will prove to you, ladies and gentlemen, that the defendant continued to drive his car along the curves of that running path—the running path that takes curves from Henderson Street to Massachusetts Avenue. A running path that goes between trees lining that running path between Henderson Street and Massachusetts Avenue.

"The impact causing Paul Mendelsohn to be hurled into the windshield of this defendant's car, on the right-hand side of the car.

"The impact, ladies and gentlemen, causing his head to go through that windshield, and you will hear that this defendant continued—continued to drive down that running path, without so much as putting a foot on the brake.

"He continued to drive down that running path, and Dr. Paul Mendelsohn was finally dumped to the ground."

Jackson paused and seemed to collect herself. "And, you will hear, ladies and gentlemen," she said, "witnesses will tell you, that this defendant continued to drive after Paul Mendelsohn was laying on the ground. He didn't stop. He continued to drive down that path, past the church, approximately three or four hundred feet.

"At approximately the same speed, this defendant continued to drive down the path.

"You will hear, ladies and gentlemen, that Deborah Brunet-Tuttle was the second individual on that path that morning.

"Deborah Brunet-Tuttle, who, at the time was thirty-one years old. She was the mother of a two year old daughter, and she was walking back from Massachusetts Avenue to her house on Matignon Road.

"She was carrying groceries, ladies and gentlemen, groceries and other items that she was going to use for the Easter Services at the Immaculate Conception Church on Alewife Brook Parkway.

"And, she'll tell you that she put those bags down as she was walking on that path. She buttoned her coat, and she looked over towards that church, and she'll tell you she never saw what hit her.

"But, what she'll tell you, ladies and gentlemen, is she felt an impact so severe, so incredible, and she'll tell you that she felt a pressure—a force, pulling at her.

"And, witnesses will tell you, ladies and gentlemen, that they heard a sound, and they looked, and they saw Deborah Brunet-Tuttle on the hood of that car, the defendant's car, and then onto the roof of the defendant's car.

"And all that time, ladies and gentlemen, this defendant continued to drive that car in a straight manner down that path, without so much as stepping on the brake, continued to drive that car.

"Deborah Brunet-Tuttle finally being hurled to the ground. And, you will hear, ladies and gentlemen that this defendant chose to continue on with Paul Mendelsohn up the path, bleeding and unconscious.

"With Deborah Brunet-Tuttle laying in a heap off the path, this defendant continued to drive up that path towards Massachusetts Avenue.

"And, in fact, ladies and gentlemen, witnesses will tell you that they even saw his car accelerate after Deborah Brunet-Tuttle was hurled from that car.

"And, that he drove that car down that path in a controlled manner, and when it got up to the point of Massachusetts Avenue, this defendant drove that car, managed to make it up that embankment onto—back onto Alewife Brook Parkway, and screech around Massachusetts Avenue, taking a right.

"Witnesses will tell you that that was the last sight they had of that car being operated. That witnesses went to the police. They went to the Cambridge Police. They went to the Arlington Police immediately afterwards, and they gave a description of the operator of the car that just ran down two people on the Alewife Brook Parkway.

"And, you'll hear from an Arlington Police Officer who will tell you that within a minute of receiving a radio dispatch, he went down Boulevard Road.

"After receiving a description of the car, a description of the operator, he went down Boulevard Road, the road we traveled this morning [during a tour of the crime scene], and he went down to the end, to Lafayette Street.

"And, down at the end of Lafayette Street, in that driveway—in a driveway, tucked in out of sight, was the car that this defendant dumped when he left the scene of Deborah Brunet-Tuttle and Paul Mendelsohn.

"That car, ladies and gentlemen, was parked," Jackson nodded knowingly. "The doors were shut. It was empty. There was no defendant at that time.

"The area was searched. The police combed the area. They combed neighborhoods. They went inside houses They searched outside of houses. They searched lawns. They searched woods.

"There was no sign of anyone fitting that driver's description.

"And, in the meantime, ladies and gentlemen, Paul Mendelsohn lay in surgery—lay in surgery attempting to sew up his head that was cut open. Attempting to stop the swelling in his brain that was rapidly increasing.

"And, Deborah Brunet-Tuttle? She, as well, lay in an emergency room with fractures all over her body, with tar embedded in her face and her arms.

"And the next time, ladies and gentlemen, that anyone heard of the operator of this car, a car that was registered to the defendant, a car that the defendant was licensed to drive, was on April 15th, the next day, thirty-six hours later. The police found out that the defendant wasn't in Massachusetts. He was now in New York, and he was safely inside a psychiatric clinic that he checked himself into in New York City.

"In the meantime, ladies and gentlemen, Paul Mendelsohn never regained consciousness. He died as a result of his fractures in his skull, and the brain swelling.

"And, Deborah Brunet-Tuttle?

"She spent two weeks in the Massachusetts General Hospital, unable to even lift herself up for most of that time.

"And, then two months in the Spaulding Rehabilitation Center, recovering from the injuries she sustained, and to this date, ladies and gentlemen, eight months later, she still suffers from those debilitating injuries that this defendant caused.'' Jackson paused again, and when she resumed, her voice was full of certainty and resolve.

"Ladies and gentlemen," she said, "the Commonwealth will prove to you that the death and the destruction that was wrought on the Alewife Brook Parkway running path, on April 14, 1990, was caused by the conscious, deliberate and intentional acts of this defendant, who made choices on that morning—choices to drive his car in a particular manner, choices to drive his car away from that scene, choices to do what, in fact, he did, by striking down two individuals.

"The Commonwealth suggests to you, ladies and gentlemen, that these acts are criminal, and that these acts are intentional, and that you hold the defendant responsible."

Defense attorney Jonathan Shapiro followed. His considered style, which some called didactic, was dramatically different from Jackson's. So, too, was his perspective on both human nature and the legal system. Unlike Jackson, who regarded violent criminals as evil people to be punished, Shapiro saw them as victims of life events beyond their control. Because of this, he considered the work of enforcing the law unpalatable.

"Human beings are pretty much alike," he told me, "and the variations of life experience that ultimately cause people to commit crimes might cause any one of us to commit them."

Having suffered his own share of bullies and anti-Semites as a boy, Shapiro came to devote his professional life to sticking up for those he considered underdogs. After graduating from Harvard Law School in 1964, he became convinced that the legal system was being manipulated to suppress the civil rights movement, and he moved to Jackson, Mississippi, to represent minority defendants in criminal cases. The experience captured him, and he went on to defend cases for the NAACP Legal Defense Fund during the late sixties and early seventies.

His work on behalf of minorities took him to the U.S. Supreme Court on multiple occasions, most notably to represent Muhammad Ali, successfully arguing that his conviction for evading the draft should be overturned. Later he founded a Boston law firm with partners who shared his passion for civil rights work.

Shapiro had come to see the entire legal system as flawed and oppressive. "The legal system," he said, "is based on the notion that there is free will and that punishing people on the basis of what they do [out of their own free will] can change their conduct and deter others. I think that's fiction." To help those at the mercy of the system, he had developed a course on prisoners' rights at the Northeastern Law School (where Kappler's daughter was a student) and had become active in programs designed to assist convicts with legal matters while in prison.

Shapiro faced a special problem in defending Kappler. Not only is the insanity defense unpopular with the public and with judges, but it demanded that he portray his client as a basically decent man sporadically commandeered by a mental illness. Only Kappler's state of mind at the moment of his crimes—*not* his underlying character structure—would be considered relevant to his guilt or innocence. This requirement effectively obscured the potential cause-and-effect link between Kappler's life and his violence.

Perhaps fearing that Kappler would not evoke sympathy, Shapiro never called him to the stand. But Kappler's self-confessed inability to show remorse—to feel the pain of his victims and their families—was some of the scarce evidence available that hinted at what he had suffered himself.

The death of a promising young physician and the continued disability of Deborah Brunet-Tuttle testified to what Kappler had taken from others. Shapiro would never succeed in conveying the pathos of what his client had lost. The heart of John Kappler's predicament, in fact, was very nearly absent from his lawyer's opening statement.

"May it please the Court, Ms. Jackson, ladies and gentlemen of the jury," Shapiro began.

"There is no question that April 14th was a terrible tragedy.

"You've heard Ms. Jackson describe it in excruciating detail. It was a tragedy for the victims, and it was a tragedy for their families.

"But, it was just as certain a tragedy for the defendant in this case, John Kappler and his family.

"As Judge Barton told you prior to your being selected as jurors in this case, there is no real dispute with respect to what happened on April 14th at approximately 10:15 or 10:30 in the morning.

"The Defendant, John Kappler, admits that he drove the car that struck Paul Mendelsohn and Deborah Brunet-Tuttle.

"He was driving. He was in that car and he drove the car in the area that we saw this morning.

"But, what you saw this morning [during the bus tour of the crime scene], although it was a pleasant outing, and an unusual break from usual courtroom routine on a pleasant day, really has very little to do with what this case is about.

"Because, what this case is about is not what happened because there is no real dispute as to what happened.

"The real question in this case is why did it happen?

"Why did John Kappler drive that car off of that Alewife Brook Parkway, and down the footpath, striking Paul Mendelsohn and Deborah Brunet-Tuttle?

"That is what, really, this case is about, and that is what most of the evidence that you will hear will be about.

"The evidence will show that John Kappler, who is a retired Medical Doctor who specialized in anesthesiology, and his wife, Tommie, left California in March of this year, to come to Medford to visit their daughter who is a law student at Northeastern.

"They drove cross country in their car, arriving in Boston—in the Boston area, in Medford, on April 11th.

"They spent the next two days sightseeing in Boston and Rockport. And, on the morning of April 14th, Dr. Kappler left to drive to New York City, where he was going to see his son, Jack, who was a student at NYU, pick up an amplifier that he was going to take back to California with him, and then go on to Washington, DC, where he was going to spend Easter with his other daughter and friends.

"Minutes after leaving the house—Elsie Kappler's house in Medford, where we went this morning, he suddenly and unpredictably turned his car off of the Alewife Brook Parkway onto the footpath, and drove down the footpath, striking the two victims in this case."

Shapiro focused intently on the jurors to highlight his central message. "It was an act without purpose," he said emphatically. "It was an act without motive. And, it was an act without reason because he had never seen or had anything to do with either of those people before.

"He had never before in his life, been in that area before. It was completely irrational, purposeless and motiveless.

"Now, Ms. Jackson says that the Commonwealth will

prove to you beyond a reasonable doubt that Dr. Kappler's act was a rational, intentional choice to kill two people, and that he acted as a cold-blooded murderer.

"I will present evidence, however, that this is not at all the case. Rather, the testimony that you will hear and it will show, I believe, that what Dr. Kappler did on the morning of April 14th was the product of a diseased mind, which made him incapable of controlling his conduct, and conforming his conduct to the requirements of the law.

"The evidence, I submit, will show to you that he did what he did because he was completely and utterly insane at the time. Because, why else would a person who had all the advantages he, his wife and his family had, who had lived and was living, a good life, why would he choose . . .

"I will present evidence of several psychiatrists and psychologists who will testify that in their opinion, on the basis of their experience, their review of the medical and hospital records, their interviews with Dr. Kappler and members of the family, the people who treated him in the past, was suffering from a severe mental illness.

"That he was suffering from a psychosis which is characterized by a loss of contact, by an individual, with reality.

"They will testify that Dr. Kappler was suffering from this mental illness, and it was a mental illness as a result of which, he would be transported into a nightmarish world, during which he believed that he was controlled by external forces, by the devil himself, and that he did what he did as a result of commands by this external force, which he was powerless to resist.

"They will testify that this form of mental illness, and this psychosis, made Dr. Kappler legally insane at the time that he committed the acts about which you will hear testimony, and that he was legally insane because, in their opinion, at the time of the acts, he was unable to appreciate, to understand the difference between right and wrong.''

Shapiro paused and turned momentarily to look at his client, whose face was a blank, then faced the jury again. ''He was unable to appreciate that what he was doing was wrong,'' he went on, ''and that he was also unable to control his conduct.

''He was powerless to resist the voice that was commanding him to follow is [*sic*] inexorable directions from that voice.''

Shapiro detailed the most dramatic of Kappler's symptoms and his various hospitalizations. But when he stated that Kappler had lost contact with reality in Chicago in 1966, Jackson, unwilling to accept that he had ever been truly psychotic, objected. The objection was overruled by Judge Barton.

In hopes of demonstrating the severity of his client's illness, Shapiro detailed Kappler's other seemingly senseless and violent acts, including trying to kill patients. He ended with Kappler's journey to Boston and New York.

''Before he left on the trip to—to come east,'' he said, ''he went to see Dr. Hyndman to ask him whether it was okay for him to make the trip.

''He talked to Dr. Hyndman, and Dr. Hyndman, he examined him, told him to make sure that he had the medication if he needed it, and it was okay to go.

''And he did. He drove cross country. And, it wasn't until, really, a few days before April 14th that he gradually began sinking into the psychotic state which was similar to what had happened in the past.

''He began experiencing delusions. He began thinking

that people were talking about him, giving him mysterious messages.

"These are signs which the psychiatrist will testify, will tell you, are typical of this kind of psychosis. They're called 'ideas of reference.' Things that don't make any sense in any kind of a rational way, but to a diseased mind, has some kind of mysterious meaning.

"He sank deeper and deeper into the psychosis until, on the morning of April 14, he was deeply into the nightmare that he believed was hell.

"He got up. He had breakfast. He left the house, and he followed the directions of the voices that told him where to drive, what to do.

"And those voices told him and directed him to turn off the Alewife Brook Parkway, and drive down that footpath, and to strike Paul Mendelsohn and Deborah Brunet-Tuttle.

"They told him to do it, and he was powerless to resist, not because he chose to do it, but because of the illness which made him powerless to do it.

"These—what he did was the result, as the witnesses who will testify before you will tell you. That he did what he did because he was, in any real sense, powerless to resist the commands.

"The voice told him to hit the victims, to go back on the road, turn on Massachusetts Avenue, and turn on Boulevard Road. To drive down the road, turn into the driveway where he saw the dog, to leave the car.

"He got out. The voice told him to remember to take his money. He got back in the car. He took his money, and he left.

"And, for the next ten hours or more, wandered aimlessly in that area and other areas where he doesn't even remember going, not seeking to leave. Not seeking to avoid discovery, because he had left the car with the registration, with identification.

"There was no rational attempt to avoid detection. In fact, Dr. Kappler walked right by the scene of the accident while the victims were still there being placed in ambulances.

"And, as he did so, deep in the nightmare of his illness, a police car went by and the siren went off, and he thought the 'woof-woof' of the siren was a congratulation to him.

"That was the depth to which he had sunk into his illness.

"Somehow during the day, after walking for miles, he wound up on Route 128 near the Mishawam Commuter Rail Station, miles from the Alewife Brook Parkway.

"He took the commuter rail downtown to North Station. He went, somehow, to the Peter Pan Bus Terminal, where he arrived about 9:00 at night. He bought a ticket. He waited around in the terminal, in full view of everybody who was there, no attempt being made to avoid detection.

"All the time, still completely delusional, hallucinating, believing the voices were directing him what to do, and where to go. Believing that things were going to happen, were happening, that had no real relationship to reality. . . .

". . . Now, ladies and gentlemen, the law draws a line between those people, on one hand, who it says should be treated as criminals because the conscious rational choices to do wrong must be punished, and those persons, on the other hand, who the law recognizes, act as a result of illness where they are no longer capable of making a conscious, rational choice.

"And, the law says that those people should not be treated as criminals, but, rather, they should be treated as mentally ill persons, and treated accordingly.

"I am sure, ladies and gentlemen, after you've heard all of the evidence in this case, that you will conclude that Dr. Kappler is of that latter category, and that his conduct on April 14th was a part of a mental disease which made him powerless to resist the inexorable commands that he was experiencing as a result of that mental illness."

Nowhere in Shapiro's opening statement did he answer his own provocative leading question: *Why did it happen?* Why did John Kappler kill Paul Mendelsohn and seriously injure Deborah Brunet-Tuttle? In clinging to the requirements of the insanity defense, in which an anonymous mental illness is to blame and one's character is not at issue, he was hamstrung by the same dilemma psychiatry itself faces. He could not capture the real story of his client using sterile clinical jargon. In the same way that biological psychiatry would leave Kappler's soul out of his own symptoms, the legal proceedings left his soul out of his own deeds.

# CHAPTER 16

The world was a loathsome thing and had to be destroyed. And anyone who had come to see that must take the last step, the very last, to the place where despair and contempt are self-throttled, where you could go no further, where you hear the Angel of the Last Day beating at the dull walls of the flesh, whither neither the light penetrated nor the darkness, but where one was alone with one's rage and could feel oneself utterly, and heighten that self and take something sacred and smash it into bits. That was it, that! To take something holy, something pure, and become master of it and grind it to the earth and stamp it out.

—Jakob Wassermann, *The World's Illusion*

On December 7, Deborah Brunet-Tuttle, a soft-spoken and highly religious young woman still healing from her injuries and using a wheelchair, began to testify.

Judge Barton tried to make Marcy Jackson stick to facts about the path Tuttle had been walking on April 14 and the mechanics of how she had been hit. He repeatedly sustained Jonathan Shapiro's objections to questions from Jackson that seemed designed to elicit evocative memories of the tragedy.

After a question that seemed to invite Tuttle to speak at some length about her three-year-old daughter, Sara Grace, Barton summoned Jackson to the side bar for a conference. "This case is to be decided without sympathy for anybody—sympathy for the defendant, sympathy for the victims," he told her flatly.

Still, it must have been hard for jurors to avoid sensing that forces of good and evil were aligned against one another that spring day. They knew Paul Mendelsohn was embarking on a career based on empathy when he was brutally killed. They heard that Tuttle was about to finish a graduate degree in human services at Lesley College in Cambridge, that she was carrying Easter eggs for a children's hunt and was walking by the church where she was planning to attend the Easter vigil service that evening.

These facts comprised a story with powerful emotional themes. "I remember the sense of impact, like being sucked into a black hole and everything just went black," Tuttle testified. ". . . I remember I couldn't remember if Sarah was with me and I remember asking and screaming, 'Where is she?' "

Good versus evil. Darkness versus light. Lawyers, like many psychiatrists, may try to insulate their fields from such subjective themes, but they are still at the center of many criminal acts and psychiatric illnesses.

Perhaps these themes gripped Kappler himself on April 14 as he began his long drive home, the broken pieces of his soul already having shred the thin mask of sanity over them. Maybe seeing a young man running strongly in the spring sun and a young woman strolling near a church just before Easter finally unleashed his rage. Maybe his motive was nothing more or less than to reproduce the wreckage of his own core self. Is it so hard to believe that their aliveness in some immeasurable way attracted his destructiveness? And could such an impulse to snuff out life have been irresistible to him?

How human a legal system can we have if, by design, it denies subjective feelings and themes? Barton's words, part and parcel of the legal process, are hard to dismiss:

"This case is to be decided without sympathy for anybody."

Despite all the Norman Rockwell–like scenes of his father's medical practice that he paints, despite his statement that he couldn't have had a better childhood, Buzz Barton gravitated away from human connections. He chose a career that incorporated a surgeon's professional distance from others, a black robe taking the place of a surgical mask. "I would have been a surgeon if I went into medicine," he told me. "The impersonal aspect of it would appeal to me."

"I'm a very emotional guy," Barton reflected, "but the only way I survive is to keep it in my family—my wife, my kids. If I let it run free and felt for everyone who came in my courtroom, I wouldn't be able to sentence anyone. I'd have a nervous breakdown."

Why should keeping his heart open drive a judge beyond his capacity for reason?

"What is the cost of doing the work you do?" I asked Barton.

"The cost is what I've become," he said simply.

At another side bar conference, Judge Barton, in partial agreement with an objection by Jonathan Shapiro, agreed to sanitize the Massachusetts General Hospital Operative Report that detailed some of the efforts to save Paul Mendelsohn's life.

"On the first page," Barton ruled, "the language 'unfortunate' is to be stricken. That obviously is somebody's opinion. It doesn't relate to the medical terminology. It reads now, 'This unfortunate, unknown male.' And there can be no question that it truly was unfortunate, but that doesn't and shouldn't appear on the hospital record. So that word will be sanitized."

\*   \*   \*

By December 11 the bulk of the factual information about what happened on April 14 had been presented to the jury by police officers and physicians. Shapiro then petitioned Barton to intervene in the judicial process and independently dismiss the three indictments against John Kappler—an action called a directed verdict. "We submit," Shapiro argued, "that there is not sufficient evidence from which a rational, fact-finder could find that, on the basis of the evidence, that the Defendant intended to kill Dr. Mendelsohn or he intended to murder Miss Brunet-Tuttle.

"And similarly, we think that the rational, fact-finder could not, on this evidence, come to the conclusion that he intended to assault and batter Miss Tuttle.

"We think that, on the whole, the evidence falls significantly short of establishing that critical mental element. The only evidence has to do with the fact of an accident. There is not sufficient evidence to find beyond that that there is a requisite mental intent.

"So, I would move at this point that so much of the indictment, as charged, is murder in the second degree, a directed verdict of acquittal be entered on so much of the indictment, as charged, and that a directed verdict of acquittal be entered on both of the other two charges."

Judge Barton thanked Shapiro and asked Jackson for her position.

"I would submit," Jackson reasoned, "that the Commonwealth has proven, beyond a reasonable doubt, in a light most favorable to the Commonwealth that this Defendant had the requisite intent to kill or intend to do an act that would cause grievous bodily harm, and intent to do an act which would create a plain and strong likelihood of grievous bodily harm.

"If Your Honor wishes, the testimony of the witnesses, as they testified during the course of the Commonwealth's case, indicated that the Defendant, who was the operator of the car, drove straight down that path without ever stopping his car, without ever putting on his brakes, drove straight into those individuals without making any attempt to swerve, avoid contact, fled from the scene, drove right into them, they suffered major injuries and death, in one case, Your Honor.

"Clearly, Your Honor, the Commonwealth has proven that this Defendant intended to commit an act that caused the plain and strong likelihood of death or grievous bodily harm.

"And for that, on second degree murder, I would suggest that the Commonwealth has, in fact, sustained its burden with assault with intent to murder and—"

Barton, not about to stop the trial, interrupted: "You needn't say any more. As far as the Defendant's Motions for a Required Finding of Not Guilty on all three indictments, that Motion is denied. The Defendant's rights are saved."

# CHAPTER 17

Tommie Kappler took the stand on December 12, a witness for the defense. Jonathan Shapiro must have hoped that she would help humanize his client. Heart-wrenching descriptions of what she and her children suffered during her husband's bouts of mental illness could provide proxy evidence of the depth of his own battles with it. A portrait might emerge of a man with deep emotional bonds to a wife and children, trying desperately to keep the family unit intact amid the tempest in his brain.

But, in fact, an opposite portrait seemed to emerge. After questioning by Shapiro largely limited to a review of Kappler's symptoms over the years, Marcy Jackson succeeded in using Tommie to suggest that a kind of characterological folie à deux—a bond of callousness or evil—was at the core of the Kapplers' marriage. The testimony helped paint him as a primarily bad, rather than sick, man.

There were no tears from Tommie, no obvious suffering, no apology to the victims. More than once, she bristled over the persistence or pace of Jackson's questions, giving the impression that she was annoyed by testifying. And she came off as entitled when the jury may well have expected her to be burdened or contrite. John Kappler, of course, had worried that he might have this effect on jurors himself.

"How many hospitals did your husband work at in his career, Mrs. Kappler?" Jackson asked.

"I have absolutely no idea," Tommie answered.

"Is it more than fifty?"

"I'm sure," she said curtly.

When Jackson asked what her husband had told her about the content of the voices he heard during the 1960s, Tommie answered, "I think you'll have to ask him."

Jackson's cynicism was like a magnifying glass through which jurors could see the details of Tommie's almost incredible notions about mental illness and personal responsibility. She established those times when Tommie had told no one at the hospitals where her husband worked that he had suffered bouts of psychosis. She pointed out that Tommie had allowed him to travel alone while ill, to remain at home alone while acting bizarrely, to return to work days after psychotic episodes. She highlighted Tommie's view of lithium as nothing more than a vitamin pill.

Jurors must have been taken aback by Tommie's seeming lack of concern about her husband's 1980 attempt on a patient's life by injecting Xylocaine.

"And, you found out that he had injected someone at that hospital?" Jackson led.

"That's right," Tommie answered.

"Did the hospital [find] out?"

"I don't think the hospital ever knew," Tommie said matter-of-factly. "Nothing happened to the patient, you understand? There was no problem. It was just something he did. The patient went home the same—"

Jackson interrupted, her voice a mixture of disbelief and resolve. The patient had nearly died, after all. "Thank you, Mrs. Kappler. Your husband injected someone with a—with some sort of medication, and you didn't call the hospital to find out what the status was of that patient?''

Tommie didn't seem to get it. ''The patient went home the next day, and there's nothing wrong—''

Another interruption from Jackson: ''Did you tell the hospital what you had known about your husband injecting them with this medication?''

''No.''

Jackson paused and shrugged her shoulders. ''Did you tell Dr. Hyndman about this?''

''My husband told Dr. Hyndman,'' Tommie replied.

''Did you speak with Dr. Hyndman about this?'' Jackson persisted.

''No.''

''You kept him at home after you found out he had injected someone with a substance, and kept him home for two months; correct?''

Shapiro finally objected.

''Objection sustained,'' Barton said. ''Save it for closing argument. That's argumentative. It's not a question.''

Judge Barton may have sensed the potential damage being done the defendant by his wife. ''By the way,'' he instructed the jurors, ''any of these questions [that] are asked have absolutely nothing to do with the character of the defendant, and don't you take any of these questions as even alluding to the character of the defendant, because the defendant's character is not in question as far as this case [which instead involved the question of insanity versus sanity] is concerned.''

Jackson began to parody the voices Kappler reported hearing, using sarcasm to challenge their existence. ''Well, there was an incident in 1975; correct?'' she asked Tommie.

''Yes,'' Tommie answered.

"And, when was that incident when your husband started hearing voices?"

"He heard voices on November the 23rd."

"Did they start before that day, to your knowledge?"

"I had heard, the day before—," Tommie started.

Jackson had been walking back toward her table but turned back abruptly. "You heard them?" she asked with feigned seriousness.

"I didn't hear," Tommie tried to explain. "I saw him when I thought he was hearing voices the day before."

"I see . . . ," Jackson said, as if appeasing a dangerous patient.

While questioning Tommie about her husband's psychiatric history, Jackson sardonically asked her to clarify her testimony. "Are these 1966 voices [you're talking about] or are these '75 voices?" she asked, then forged on to inquire about the voices in 1985 when Kappler had been accused of unplugging Ben Wytewa's respirator. "And, at that time in 1985, that was also as a result of voices telling him what to do?" she asked.

"Yes," Tommie said.

"And, he told you about these voices; correct?"

"Yes. I don't know—it's not 'voices,' it's a voice," Tommie replied.

Jackson took the gift. "One voice?" she followed up.

"Well, I mean, one voice at a time," Tommie stumbled. "He only hears one voice at a time."

"Are there different voices at different times, Mrs. Kappler?" Jackson continued.

"Well, you'd have to ask him that."

"Well, do you know anything about that, Mrs. Kappler? Has he ever shared that with you?"

Tommie sounded evasive. "I've never delved into it a lot," she said.

It doesn't take much doubt in a juror's mind to derail

WITHOUT MERCY • 165

a plea of not guilty by reason of insanity. Hints that Kappler and his wife might be engaged in a cover-up of any kind could doom his defense.

"I see," Jackson nodded knowingly. "Did Dr. Kappler have any connection to this individual at all in 1985?"

"In what way do you mean?" Tommie asked.

"Did he know who this person was in 1985?"

"It was not his patient. Somebody had asked him to check on that patient that had been a nurse at that hospital."

"So, he knew who this patient was?"

"He knew his name," Tommie said, "but he didn't know the patient at all. The patient was a vegetable. I mean, he was not—he was just lying there."

With Tommie already having described a cardiac arrest precipitated by her husband as "no problem" and a paralyzed patient as "a vegetable," the jury heard that she had not only failed to tell police about the telephone message her husband had left her after killing Paul Mendelsohn but had given them an incorrect description of him.

"The police came—Mrs. Kappler, the police came to your daughter's house at around—or spoke to your daughter around 2:00 in the afternoon; is that correct?" Jackson asked.

"They spoke to me and my daughter, yes," Tommie agreed.

"And, then they came over to your house shortly after that?"

"Yes."

Jackson now turned from inquisitive to accusatory: "And, you didn't tell police at that time that your husband had called and left a message, did you?"

"They did not ask that," Tommie replied blankly.

"They told you, did they not, Mrs. Kappler, that your husband—that they thought your husband had been involved in an incident which left people injured on the Alewife Brook Parkway—''

"No."

"—isn't that correct?''

"No,'' Tommie said, "That's not exactly what they said.'' Seeking shelter in the wording of the question did not enhance her credibility.

"Well, did you—were you made aware that your husband—at that time, the police were looking for your husband because an incident occurred on the Alewife Brook Parkway?''

Tommie still wouldn't give a complete answer. "They were trying to determine if that was him,'' she said.

Jackson let her frustration show. "They were looking for him, as well, weren't they, Mrs. Kappler?''

"Yes.''

"Yet, you didn't tell them at that time that he had called; correct?''

"I was very upset—''

"Mrs. Kappler, can you answer—''

Judge Barton intervened. "Wait,'' he said to Tommie. "Go ahead and answer the question.'' Then he glanced over at Jackson. "But, she's not on trial, by the way.''

By the end of Tommie's testimony, Jackson had seriously eroded her credibility and cast real doubt on the idea that she had reliably observed anything like an anonymous major mental illness gripping her husband. Jackson ended her questioning with a kind of grand finale in which the acts of John Kappler on April 14 were reviewed yet again.

"Did he tell you he—did he tell you whether or not the voices told him to kill anyone, Mrs. Kappler?'' Jackson asked.

Again Tommie's answer sounded evasive. "He told me that the voices told him to go off that Parkway.''

"Did they tell you—did he tell you that the voices told him to drive his car into someone?"

"He said the voices—I can't remember the precise thing. They just said, 'Hit.' You know."

"And, did the—did he tell you that the voices told him what Parkway to go off of?"

"No, because I don't think he knew the name of the Parkway. He just said that the voices told him to drive off into this park."

"And, did the voices tell him to hit more than one people or person?"

"You know, Ms. Jackson, I just really don't remember what the voices said," Tommie sparred. "That wasn't what was in my mind. I can't truly remember exactly what the voices said."

But Jackson was relentless. "So, he didn't tell you that the voices—he told you some things about the voices that you can remember, and some things you can't?"

"Ms. Jackson, at that point, I was very upset, and I can't truly say what he said the voices said. . . ."

". . . Did you speak to him at some later date about what he told you the voices told him to do?"

"Yes."

"And, did he tell you that the voices told him to drive around the corner of Massachusetts Avenue after striking two people?"

"That's right. He just said—"

"And did he tell you—"

Barton broke in. "Go ahead," he directed Tommie. "Finish the answer."

"He said the voices told him to go park the car, and get out, and to walk around," Tommie finished. "And the voices told him to do some other things after that, too."

"Did the voices tell him to kill himself?" Jackson asked.

"I mean, not then. The voices didn't tell him to kill himself then."

"So," Jackson persisted, "when did the voices tell him to kill himself?"

"I don't know that the voices ever told him to kill himself," Tommie admitted. "He tried to, but I don't remember whether he was doing that by voice command or what. I don't know."

Jackson shrugged and shook her head. "Well—but you do know that the voices were commanding him to do those other things?"

"That's right."

"And, that's based on what he told you?" she confirmed.

"Yes."

"And, you don't know whether the voices were telling him to attempt suicide; correct?"

"Well, see," Tommie tried to explain, "this happened the next day. I just don't know because I didn't ask him. It hasn't come up until now."

Jackson was ready to make her point. "You only know what your husband has told you about these voices; correct?"

"Yes," Tommie said.

# CHAPTER 18

In another effort to establish that Kappler was a warm and decent family man besieged by a destructive illness, Jonathan Shapiro called Jack Kappler to the stand next. Jack was short and wiry and bore a striking resemblance to his father. He was nineteen at the time and a sophomore at New York University.

"Jack is very tense," his former roommate Stephen Feiven told me. "If you touch him, he's hard. You can feel the energy going through him." He recalled that Jack had never put any posters on the walls of his room at college because he had never found anything he considered perfect.

"[His] real name is John," Feiven said. "He changed his name to break away."

Shapiro's tone was kind, even fatherly, as he questioned Jack, but the answers he got sometimes sounded mechanical.

"Are you related to the family of John Kappler?" Shapiro asked.

"Yes, I am," Kappler responded.

"What is that relationship?"

"I am the son," Kappler said flatly, in a peculiar turn

of phrase, offered without emotion, that objectified his connection with his father. He could have said, *He is my father*, or *I am his son*.

Shapiro had Jack recount how he had searched for his father, found him in the New York Hospital emergency room, and then been attacked by him.

"Well, I was—there were two benches in the room, he was sitting on one, I was sitting on the other," Jack recalled. "And I was, you know, talking to talk, not to say anything in particular, he wasn't listening anyway; and he jumped up, and he shouted, you know, 'Okay, okay'— he had been quivering and shaking for awhile—and he jumped up and said, 'Okay, okay,' and he jumped at me, with his hands outstretched at my neck. . . . I backed up and leaned my feet in the air, and I started to kick him in the solar plexus . . . over and over again, and he still kept coming at me."

"Did he say anything?" Shapiro asked.

"No."

"Did you see his face?"

"Yes."

"Describe the appearance of his face."

"He was just blank," Kappler responded. "There was no expression at all. He just—it was blank."

Jack testified to having screamed for help and having watched his father restrained by security guards.

The story was a dramatic one, and it illustrated how bizarre—how crazy—John Kappler's behavior seemed to his son that April night. But on cross-examination, in a this-doesn't-add-up tone, Marcy Jackson raised questions about whether Kappler was truly out of control. "Now, you saw your father, and he wasn't in any sort of physical restraint when you saw him in the clinic at that time, is that correct?" she asked.

"No," Jack responded. "No, he wasn't."

"And you were able to go up to him and sit him down, and talk to him about what had happened, and where he had been, isn't that correct?"

"Yes. . . ."

"And he said he hit those people on the path point?" Jackson asked.

"No," Jack said. "Not in those exact words."

"Words to that effect, sir?"

Judge Barton cautioned her not to ask the witness for opinions.

"He said voices 'made me do it,' " Jack offered.

Jackson sensed another opportunity: "Did he say what the voices made him do, sir?"

"He went into detail for a long time."

Barton tried to make Jack clarify his answer. "Do what?" he asked. "What did he say?"

"Do it," Jack said. "Quote, do it, unquote."

"He didn't give you anymore [*sic*] details of what exactly these voices made him do?" Jackson persisted.

"Yes, he did."

"What did he say?"

"He said the voices made him walk around; he said the voices made him get a bus ticket; the voices led him around New York all day."

"What about, sir, did he give you any details about what these voices made him do on April 14, 1990 after he left your sister's house in Medford?"

"No." Jack said.

"Did he mention any of that?"

"No. Well, no. Not—no."

". . . He didn't mention any details about that. Is it fair to say he mentioned details about everything else but that?"

Jonathan Shapiro jumped to his feet to object. The objection was sustained.

"So he told you," Jackson went on, "the first thing he told you is 'the voices made me do it,' and then he told you what he did after the voices made him do it; is that correct?"

Jack seemed evasive. He mumbled his response.

Barton prodded him along. "Sir—"

"That's a 'yes,' " Jack said.

Jackson's questions were designed to make jurors wonder why Kappler didn't mention having hit two people with his car. Still in the grip of a supposed psychosis that would lead him to attempt to strangle his son, he seemed to have neatly talked around his crime. Didn't that glaring omission indicate that he knew what he did was wrong or illegal, even if he was hearing voices?

Jackson then went on to imply that Kappler might even have staged his clinical presentation at Payne Whitney. "When he was in that psychiatric hospital there were staff members from the hospital who were present while you were with him, isn't that correct, at least part of the time?" she asked.

"Technically, the whole time," Jack answered.

"And he did things during this whole time that appeared bizarre to you; is that a fair statement?"

"Yes."

"And during this whole time he did things that appeared weird to you; is that a fair statement?"

"Yes."

"And there were people around from the psychiatric hospital while he was doing these bizarre or weird things?"

"Yes, some of the time."

Jackson nodded knowingly. She hoped jurors would question whether Kappler had tried to appear crazy that night. How, they might wonder, could he have been well enough to talk in detail about the voices he had heard yet sick enough to have continued responding to them?

"He was able to relate to you the facts concerning his illness and his symptoms; is that correct?" she asked for emphasis.

"Yes," Jack said.

# CHAPTER 19

Jonathan Shapiro called highly esteemed forensic psychiatrist Dr. Martin Kelly, associate professor and associate director of psychiatry at Harvard's Brigham and Women's Hospital, as his first expert witness. Just hours before, he had finally handed Jackson volumes of medical records on Kappler that had been previously unavailable to her.

Near fifty years old, Kelly looked and sounded at home in psychiatry and the law. Tall and physically substantial, with gold wire-rimmed glasses and layered white hair, he was a study in authority. His voice had presence in it but no arrogance. Jurors heard that his qualifications as an expert witness included having evaluated over 150 accused killers and having testified in as many as 100 murder trials across the country.

He had interviewed John Kappler twice and Tommie Kappler once, spoken by telephone with Dr. Hyndman, and reviewed Kappler's medical records from 1966 through his recent stay at New York's Payne Whitney Clinic.

Before Kelly offered his opinions, Judge Barton orally reviewed the legal test of insanity in the Commonwealth of Massachusetts. "A person is considered not responsible for criminal conduct if at the time of such conduct as a result of mental disease or defect he lacks substantial capacity either to appreciate the criminality, which is the wrongfulness of his conduct, or to conform his conduct to the requirements of the law," he reminded the jury.

Shapiro began his questioning in a tone respectful of Kelly's credentials. "What is your opinion," he asked Kelly, "as to what disease or defect Doctor Kappler is suffering from?"

". . . Well, it is my belief . . . ," Kelly said, "that Doctor Kappler has had a psychotic disorder going back clearly until 1965, '66, and probably back to the mid '50s, by his own convincing description of it, of major breaks with reality."

Like John Foehl at McLean Hospital, Kelly believed Kappler was usually significantly sicker than he appeared. "It is a psychosis that's in my view always just below the surface," he explained, "and at times breaks through in ways which are obvious to other people . . . which is called 'manic' at some times, 'schizophrenic' at other times. And I am a little reluctant to either call it schizophrenic or manic because it has features of both and has a kind of chronicity in between times that may make it what we call an atypical psychosis. But unlike orthopedics where you can put up an x-ray and say it's that bone which is cracked exactly there, in psychiatry it's more descriptive.

"So that I would describe a chronic psychotic condition with various acute decompensations going back probably to 1953, but certainly '65, six, seven, '75, six, '80, '81, '84, '85 and presently having major flareups which bring them to the attention of people."

Shapiro clearly had Harvard on his side. "Can you describe the particular nature of the thought processes that occur during these decompensation periods?'' he asked.

Marcy Jackson objected. She didn't believe Kelly could know the true nature of John Kappler's thoughts, especially in the past. Her position, after all, was that Kappler was a psychopath lying about his thoughts in order to get away with murder.

Judge Barton overruled her objection.

Kelly paused a few moments, seeming a bit surprised at the interruption. ''Well, the onset for him appears to be characterized by misperceptions of reality, or misinterpretations of ordinary conversations,'' he said.

''An example of it. . . . He was in the process of traveling up the east coast, he had stopped along the way to visit people, and had occasion to have conversations with people in a cafeteria. A person mentioned that they were from Exeter—Exeter. So he heard the word 'Exeter,' and started to ponder on that word, and then thought 'exit her,' in the sense of the red sign on the doors, 'exit her,' and then started to have all kinds of meanings. And he thought it meant his wife would have to die and maybe he would have to kill her.

''He has been through these episodes before enough to know that if he were to say that to his wife, she would say, 'I think you're getting sick again, I think we need to get some medical or psychiatric attention.' So in his psychotic state he still is able to, particularly at the beginning, cover it up, conceal it from other people.

''But the beginning part in this instance, and in his description of some other incidentals, is to start to misinterpret ordinary conversations, ordinary bits of—He sees someone on the ward and they have longish hair, and somebody else has long hair but not quite as long, so he then gets into a system whereby he believes there is a hierarchy in this psychiatric ward that somehow has to do with the length of the hair of the individual. So that he develops these kinds of notions, he doesn't tell people them, because he knows that other people are going to regard that sort of thing as, quote, crazy. . . .

"And his thoughts then take on a kind of life of their own, he becomes preoccupied with various kinds of things. And eventually in most instances it has spilled into behavior which is obviously out of keeping, running out in the middle of the night, and getting into his car, and driving off and getting into an accident with no particular place to go. Those kinds of things. . . .

". . . He is now able to look back, but he can describe what he was thinking at the time from the position now of a historian, an observer, looking back basically on his own behavior. And he basically describes being terrorized, being fragmented, being desperate, internally, and that he lost control of his own thought processes, and that it was very, very painful to him.

"He was, basically, suffering, and in certain instances driven to walk around, or to pace around, or to do certain kinds of acts. Many of the situations have involved a phenomenon which happens in some psychoses of commands, 'Get out of here,' 'Get in a car,' 'Take this turn,' those kinds of things. . . .

". . . In Doctor Kappler's case I believe he has command hallucinations and describes them in ways that are familiar to me."

In speaking of Kappler's suffering, Kelly had finally begun to humanize him. Shapiro walked closer to the jury, then addressed him:

"So, are Doctor Kappler's descriptions of these command hallucinations that he experienced in the past consistent with what is experienced by . . . patients with psychotic disorders?"

"Correct," Kelly said.

Jackson objected, albeit too late, to Shapiro's question

because it presumed that Kappler had, in fact, experienced hallucinations. Judge Barton again overruled her.

"Let me ask you this," Shapiro went on. "You mentioned the occasion in which he described the word 'exit,' does that have a particular [scientific] term in the literature?"

"It is [called] an idea of reference . . . ," Kelly answered with confidence. "He had a delusion that there was some special meaning to that versus someone saying 'I am from Exeter.' So that's a delusion that is a part of, component part, almost essential part of any psychotic disorder. And it is an idea of reference in the sense that this person was saying to me, this was specifically referential, it was specifically meant for me to hear, 'all of this exists in this way for me.' "

"In view of your opinion as to the fact that Doctor Kappler is suffering from a psychotic disorder, how do you account for the fact that over the course of the last twenty to thirty years he has been able to function apparently normally for long periods of time?"

"Objection," Jackson interrupted. She wanted the record to register her repeated resistance to the "fact" that Kappler suffered from psychosis.

"Overruled," Barton said. "Go ahead, Doctor."

Kelly nodded his thanks to the judge. "Well, when he is not in the midst of an acute decompensation he is particularly good at concrete kinds of things, things that are basically right in front of him and don't require a great deal of ambiguity," he explained to Shapiro. "He also is a very, very intelligent person who probably conceals even from members of the family his disturbance. . . . He is generally on his own guard and working very hard with his intellect to keep things in order, and by and large does a pretty good job except when it breaks through to the surface."

"Do you have an opinion as to the reason why in the past the psychotic disorder has on various occasions broken through?" Shapiro queried.

"Objection," Jackson said emphatically.

"Overruled," Barton responded.

"It is the nature of the psychotic conditions," Kelly went on, "that probably have at least some biological components that they just break through from time to time. The nature of a disorder, like manic depressive illness, or schizophrenic, and he's been called both, is that a person may be going along fairly well and it's usually not in response to stress or a life situation. . . .

"Now stress may have some role in making it happen today rather than tomorrow, but I could not find any particular pattern in his life, nor is it generally true in my view, that psychotic decompensations follow life events. . . . It's somewhat like diabetes, which even though things are in pretty good control, a person is watchful of their diet and exercise, and things of that sort, the illness can flare up."

Using a writing tablet to illustrate the dates and circumstances of Kappler's previous hospitalizations, Kelly tried to explain away the variety of diagnoses Kappler had received. He knew, of course, that patients can be assigned one or another diagnosis depending on the clinician—or the times. "The precise diagnosis, if you will, in the task that I am asked to perform, is less critical," he said. "That may be a very interesting discussion among psychiatrists . . . [but] it's clear to everyone that it's a psychotic disorder."

Shapiro was more than satisfied. He was now ready for the doctor's opinions about Kappler's mental state the day he killed Paul Mendelsohn.

"Now, Doctor Kelly," he asked, "turning your attention from whether or not Doctor Kappler is suffering presently and has suffered in the past from the mental disease or defect, did you form an opinion as to whether he was suffering from a mental disease or defect at the time of the incident on April 14, 1990?''

"Yes, I did.''

"What is that opinion?''

"That he was suffering from [the] mental disease or defect on that date.''

"Can you describe,'' Shapiro asked, "what it is about Doctor Kappler's description of what happened that leads you to conclude that that is consistent with a person who is suffering from the kind of mental disease that you have described?''

"Well, here we have someone who is looking back and trying to describe to another person how he thought when he was psychotic. . . . That whole process of describing the days prior to the situation [the alleged murder], the, basically, command hallucinations around the time of the accident, and the period afterwards, in terms of his own description, was familiar and compelling to me in terms of, yes, this is the description after the fact of someone commenting on their own psychotic state.''

"Is it [in] any way unusual for somebody who has been in a psychotic state to be able to describe that state at some later time?''

"Well, it's a little complicated in that the person is now rational, trying to describe the irrational. And when you try to do that you almost make it seem more orderly than it is to the person while they are experiencing, basically, the fragmentation and disruption of their thoughts.

". . . I think he genuinely tried to recall as much as he could. And his own kind of personality style is to be very precise, detailed, and it was like it was important to him to tell every element of it, and he could keep track of every element of it much better than I could in listening.''

Anticipating Jackson's position that Kappler was lying about his symptoms, Shapiro then asked Kelly directly whether he believed the defendant was being honest with him.

"My impression was that he was attempting to be co-operative and candid," Kelly said. "I didn't think that he was trying to deceive me. That was not my impression."

Shapiro knew that Kelly didn't think his client had lost his ability to tell right from wrong when he struck Mendelsohn and Tuttle, so he focused his next question on whether Kappler had the capacity to resist doing wrong.

"Doctor Kelly," he asked, "do you have . . . an opinion . . . as to whether or not at the time of the incident, on April 14, 1990, Doctor Kappler had substantial capacity to conform his conduct to the requirements of the law?"

"Yes, I do," Kelly nodded.

"What is that opinion?" Shapiro led.

"That he did not have the capacity to conform his conduct to the requirements of the law. His conduct was being controlled, directed, driven, shaped by the psychotic state that he was in."

Shapiro looked over at the jury and kept looking at them as he asked his next question: "Can you explain why you came to that conclusion?"

"Well, I think he has a clear past history of psychotic disorders," Kelly said. "I believe he was acutely psychotic at the time. His description made sense to me, it was familiar to me. And the act itself has almost no sensible basis in reality.

"This was not a situation in which he even knew either of the victims; there is no possibility of gain, it's not like robbing a bank or doing some other kind of illegal act that has some at least plausible advantage to the individual. . . .

"I happen to believe he was responding to literally command hallucinations to turn left, turn right, do this, do that; but he was in the midst of a delusional system, at any rate, which would have been sufficient in any view to meet the criteria psychiatrically of losing the capacity to conform conduct to the requirement of the law."

Having gotten an unambiguous exoneration of his client from one of the top psychiatrists in America, Shapiro turned Kelly over for cross-examination. But Jackson had received the medical records on Kappler, hundreds of pages long, just that day and asked Judge Barton for time to review them.

He called her to the bench. "Let me tell you something," he said quietly. "I will give you that opportunity until 9:30 tomorrow morning. From now on, any psychiatric witness that comes on, you are going right forward with him. Do you understand?"

Jackson wasn't intimidated. "I have until 9:30, that's the latest, tomorrow, under those conditions?" she bristled.

"No question about it," Barton said flatly.

"Okay," Jackson said. She started to walk away but turned back. ". . . Perhaps in the middle of tomorrow morning," she said.

Barton grinned slightly. "9:30 tomorrow morning," he repeated.

# CHAPTER 20

**M**arcy Jackson had no expert in psychiatry who would testify that Kappler was undoubtedly sane at the time he veered off the Alewife Brook Parkway. Tyler Carpenter and Fred Kelso would raise the possibility that Kappler sometimes faked his symptoms, but neither had absolutely ruled out the possibility that on April 14 Kappler was hopelessly in the grip of psychosis.

With the tide of expert opinion likely to run against her case, Jackson made a critical decision: She resolved to put the field of psychiatry itself on the witness stand.

Through sleepless nights she had read and reread the 567-page American Psychiatric Association's *Diagnostic and Statistical Manual* (DSM III-R). She had grilled psychiatrists she knew not only on the clinical signs and symptoms of the conditions listed but on how reliably the conditions could be differentiated from one another. And she had become convinced that psychiatric diagnoses were so mired in ambiguity and inconsistency that jurors could be moved to discount the expert opinions they would hear.

In particular, Jackson believed she could successfully

argue that the bulk of Kappler's symptoms better fit the diagnostic criteria for antisocial personality disorder than any major psychotic illness. In other words, she would show that Kappler was a pure psychopath. She called David Marks, a gifted assistant district attorney, and asked that he come by and help prepare her for Kelly's cross-examination. She went straight from the courthouse to her office.

For some time, Jackson had wondered whether the life of a litigator was really for her, had even thought of leaving the law entirely. But that night there was no ambivalence in her mind. Judge Barton's authoritarian, slightly dismissive tone with her had challenged, and thereby renewed, her vision of herself as a fierce competitor. She poured herself a cup of coffee, spread Kappler's medical records across a conference table, and began to comb through them.

At precisely 9:30 A.M. on December 14, Dr. Martin Kelly took the stand for his cross-examination.

Jackson had had little sleep, but she didn't feel tired. Within a minute of beginning her questioning, she was at the heart of her argument. There was nothing of Shapiro's reverence for experts in her tone.

"Doctor Kelly," she started, "are you familiar with the manual, DSM III-R?"

Asking the associate director of psychiatry at the Brigham and Women's Hospital if he was familiar with the DSM III-R was like asking the pope if he was familiar with the Bible.

"Yes, I am," he replied curtly.

"Do you know what that is, sir?" she persisted.

"Yes, I do."

"It's fair to say it's a recognized diagnostic manual

used by individuals like yourself to formulate diagnoses?''

"Yes, it is."

"And it's in fact used by, is it fair to say, it's used by just about every single . . . [psychiatrist] in formulating a diagnosis.''

In reply, Kelly tried to explain psychiatry's somewhat schizophrenic view of its own diagnostic manual. "Probably that's not accurate," he said. "It is a manual that codes various diagnoses. And it's essential if you're submitting a bill to an insurance company that you refer to those. But for the most part—well, in teaching-kind of settings I don't particularly like it, and in certain kinds of practice, psychoanalytic practice, or cognitive therapy practice it's not used. But it is the official diagnostic scheme of the American Psychiatric Association.''

Kelly's opinion of DSM III-R—that it is as much an economic as a scientific work, an overzealous attempt to label people with conditions that insurance companies will pay to treat—is widely held. The book is, in fact, shunned by some gifted teachers who, like Kelly, are still more focused on understanding the suffering of patients than naming it.

But Jackson knew that jurors might not abide the inconsistency. She paused and nodded slowly for effect, as if to highlight the fact that the manual was an official document but one Kelly didn't always stick to. "And your diagnosis, Doctor Kelly, is, what I believe you said yesterday, chronic psychotic condition?'' she asked.

"That's correct.''

"That's not in DSM III-R as a diagnosis, is it . . . sir, as a diagnosis of a mental disease or defect?''

"Not as such. What [I] meant by—''

Jackson cut him off. She intended to hold him to the confines of the DSM III-R. "Now is it fair to say, sir, that this is a condition, or a diagnosis that you made that is not one that comes up regularly until [you are retained for] your evaluations for criminal responsibility?''

"Psychosis?" Kelly shrugged. "Comes up very regularly."

"[I mean] this chronic psychotic condition, as you stated," Jackson persisted.

"I didn't mean it to be in capitals," Kelly protested. "I was describing conditions. In my view, Doctor Kappler has a chronic psychotic condition with acute flare-ups. He has been called manic-depressive, schizophrenic. My diagnosis would be atypical psychotic condition, which is in the book. That degree of specificity, I think, didn't—that precision I didn't think was necessary."

Jackson looked at Kelly as if he was either hopelessly confused or naive. This was a murder trial, after all. When would precision be more crucial? "Atypical means you don't really know what it is, you can't put a name on it?" she baited him.

The doctor found himself face-to-face with modern psychiatry's peculiar diagnostic dialect. "No," Kelly said. "It means it is not atypical bipolar manic depressive disorder and it's not atypical schizophrenic."

"Atypical psychosis means it doesn't have any of the characteristics that are pinned into any particular type of mental disease or defect?" Jackson prodded.

"It has some of them, but it might not meet all the criteria for a pure manic depressive bipolar disorder or a pure schizophrenic."

"It's somewhat of a . . . [melting] pot, is that fair to say?"

"To some degree."

Jackson was pacing in front of the jury. She hoped they were losing confidence not just in Kelly but in the entire field of psychiatry. She stopped and looked directly at him. "You don't know for sure what . . . [Kappler's] mental disease or defect is?" she asked.

"That's not correct," Kelly protested, trying to stay in control. "I know for sure that he has a psychotic condition, chronically, with acute exacerbations. I know that for sure."

"And it's atypical melting pot, correct?" Jackson said wryly.

"The best diagnosis in that book I have problems with is atypical psychotic disorder. That's the best one, in my opinion."

"But you don't know exactly what this defendant suffers from if he suffers from any at all, isn't that correct?"

Kelly's frustration showed. "I don't know how to respond to that question. I tried to say what my diagnosis is. In terms of exactly, 'exactly,' I don't know what you mean particularly by that."

"Well, the defendant's symptoms, his characteristics that you noted, those are consistent with other diagnoses in DSM III-R, is that correct?"

"Which symptoms?"

"Some of the symptoms he has . . ."

"Hallucinations and delusions can be found in manic depressive disorder, schizophrenia, other psychotic conditions. . . ."

Jackson was now ready to advance her own clinical theory about Kappler: "What I am referring to, Doctor, are other . . . diagnoses in DSM III-R, such as having a personality disorder?"

"I think I said it is possible to have both a personality disorder and to have schizophrenia," Kelly said. ". . . The diagnosis that was relevant to the issue of his criminal responsibility was a psychotic condition, but he might have a personality disorder as well."

"Doctor Kelly," Jackson said, "some of the characteristics for an antisocial personality would be before the age of fifteen when an individual initiates a physical fight, is that correct?''

''That could be a criteria [*sic*]. I'm not aware that's true of Doctor Kappler.''

Jackson established that Kelly had reviewed Fred Kelso's report on Kappler, then picked the report off her desk. ''On page 7, of Doctor Kelso's report . . . the defendant states: When he was eight or nine years old he often would pummel the hell out of a kid who was chasing him in his backyard at his father's direction; do you recall that?'' she asked.

''. . . My recollection of that page,'' Kelly argued, ''is that he didn't particularly want to be in fights, but his father was bringing kids to his backyard to encourage him to fight with the kids to toughen himself up. . . .''

''Are you familiar with another characteristic of an antisocial personality when an individual deliberately destroys other people's property?''

''That can be a characteristic.''

''Are you familiar as well with Doctor Kelso's report on page 7 where the defendant tells him that he stole a car, and then he eventually rode it all over town, and eventually wrecked it in a funeral home, when he was fifteen?''

''I don't have a specific recollection of that.''

''Do you have a recollection, sir, about the defendant telling Doctor Kelso, as well, on page 7 of his report, that he got into trouble when he was using a bulldozer that was across the street and moving it around; do you recollect anything like that?''

''Vaguely.''

''Do you also remember anything about the defendant telling Doctor Kelso about throwing tomatoes at a bar and getting caught and getting in trouble for that, when he was around fourteen?''

''I don't have a specific recollection of that.''

''Mr. Foreman, ladies and gentlemen of the jury,'' Judge Barton broke in. He recognized that Jackson was succeeding in introducing the issue of character by confronting an expert witness about his diagnostic impressions of Kappler. She was skillfully using the DSM III-R criteria for antisocial personality disorder to track Kappler's darker side back to his youth. ''I emphasize again, none of this comes in for the truth of the matters contained therein, and you are not to consider it in any way as evidence of his character or propensity to commit crime as far as this defendant is concerned. It's only admissible as it relates to this psychiatrist or other doctors' opinions, as to the mental condition of the defendant and for no other reason.''

But how could jurors disregard the portrait Jackson was painting? She pressed on. ''What about the characteristics in an antisocial personality before age fifteen of lying; is that one of the characteristics?''

''It can be, yes,'' Kelly said.

''And do you recall the defendant telling Doctor Kelso that he lied as a child?''

''I don't have a specific recollection of that. But most children from time to time lie.''

''Do you recall him telling Doctor Kelso, 'God knows I have lied'?''

''I don't have a recollection of that.''

''Did you read this report, Doctor?'' Jackson asked provocatively.

''Yes, I did,'' Kelly answered shortly.

''. . . Are you also familiar with the characteristics of antisocial personality, before the age of fifteen, the characteristic of stealing property?''

"That can be a characteristic. . . ."

"Do you recall the defendant, on page 7, telling Doctor Kelso that he stole bottles as a child?"

"I don't have a specific recollection of that."

"What about stealing supplies from someone else and then selling them; do you recall him telling Doctor Kelso that?"

"I recall the general description of an impoverished background of a family that was sort of struggling in urban circumstances, and was not particularly supportive, and that Doctor Kappler was the first one in his family to go to high school," Kelly said. "And he had a pattern which I didn't regard as indicative of an antisocial personality disorder but of growing up in modest circumstances."

"What about stealing a car, sir, do you recall him saying that he stole a car before he was the age of fifteen, or fifteen?"

"I have no specific recollection of that item in the Kelso report," Kelly said.

Jackson was on to Kappler's work history within minutes. Debating the wide range of symptoms of antisocial personality disorder allowed her to introduce topics that would normally have been considered irrelevant.

"What about the characteristics of an antisocial personality [that] after you reach the age of eighteen, after you have grown up . . . that you are unable to sustain consistent work behavior?" she asked.

"That can be," Kelly granted her. "It doesn't apply to Doctor Kappler."

"Were you familiar with a job in Chicago with a pharmaceutical company which lasted only a few weeks?"

"Because he became psychotic," Kelly said.

"Were you familiar with that?"

"Yes."

"You are also familiar with the jobs, the freelance jobs, in fifty different hospitals, approximately; are you familiar with that?"

". . . I don't recall it was in the order of fifty, but . . ."

"Are you familiar with him leaving work in 1985 and not working since that time?"

"Yes, I am."

"And you are also familiar with him leaving work in 1980, saying he had hepatitis; are you familiar with that incident?"

By this point, Kelly seemed a bit worn down. "Perhaps you could refresh my memory," he said. "I know he had some troubles around 1980, '81."

"Do you recall an incident . . . cracking up a car and then going home and staying home, leaving his job and saying he had hepatitis?"

Shapiro finally objected to the wide swath Jackson was cutting through his client's life.

"Overruled," Barton said.

"I don't have a specific recollection of that . . . ," Kelly answered.

"So he didn't tell you that?" Jackson prodded.

"We didn't get into it."

Jackson was ready to journey further into Kappler's darkness. "Now, is another characteristic of an antisocial personality someone who fails to conform to social norms with respect to lawful behavior?"

"Yes, it can be," Kelly agreed.

"Would shutting off the life support system of an individual satisfy that characteristic?"

"It could."

"And would injecting patients with medications that are harmful to them satisfy that characteristic?"

"It could."

"And would driving cars into people satisfy that characteristic?"

"Yes. It could."

With Tommie Kappler's detached testimony still relatively fresh in jurors' minds, Jackson used Kelly's status as an expert to introduce the defendant's own lack of empathy. "Do you recall Doctor Kelso asking the defendant . . . about his sense of having no shame then and no shame now?"

"Maybe if you would give me back the report," Kelly surrendered.

Jackson walked over to Kelly and handed him the report. She returned to her desk and waited a brief time. Then; "All set?"

"Yes."

"Does that refresh your memory, Doctor Kelly, as to whether the defendant said he had no shame then and no shame now?"

"That sentence refers back to something that must have been earlier in the report about it, 'I asked him to tell me more about having no shame then or now.' I don't recall where that had come up earlier in the report."

"In fact, Doctor Kelly, Metropolitan State Hospital, after this incident . . . diagnosed the defendant as having a personality disorder as one of their diagnoses, as one being antisocial, narcissistic, compulsive—"

When Kelly seemed at a loss for the reference, Jackson carried another medical record over to him. "Doctor Kelly," she went on, "does that refresh your memory as to whether or not in October of 1990 Metropolitan Hospital diagnosed this defendant as having . . . a personality disorder with antisocial, narcissistic and obsessive compulsive traits?"

"Yes, it does." Kelly said.

"That's in fact one of the diagnoses, isn't that correct?"

"It is. Personality disorder, NOS, 'not otherwise specified,' and in parentheses it also has 'atypical psychosis.' "

"That melting pot, is that correct?" Jackson smiled.

"It is a diagnosis in the DSM III-R, it is a fair diagnosis, actually, in this case."

Jackson ignored Kelly's point. "Now the defendant's history, his prior acts and not just his words, in fact, Doctor, meet some of the specifications of a personality disorder?"

"Some."

"And a personality disorder isn't recognized as a mental disease or defect which is sufficient to satisfy the requirements of . . . [an insanity defense], correct?"

"Generally, I don't. But maybe some courts would have, I don't know."

"Antisocial personality disorder would not, though?"

"Generally not, no."

Jackson had made significant strides toward depositing Kappler in the psycho-judicial no-man's-land of character disorders. The ways in which his tortured past might have warped his personality wouldn't weigh in on the side of innocence. That brand of *mad*ness was outside the bounds of the insanity defense.

Capitalizing on the ground she had gained, Jackson proceeded to question whether Kappler really suffered from anything beyond a personality disorder.

"Now, in order to reach your opinion that the defendant has this condition [atypical psychosis], as you call it, you rely in large part on the defendant's statements that he had these auditory hallucinations, correct?"

"In some part, yes," Kelly said.

"Well, you must believe, in fact, if you rely on them,

that what he tells you is the truth?''

"To some degree. You would look for other confirming evidence, but . . . since you can't hear the voice, you do rely on the person's report of that.''

"There is no way to verify that a person actually hears these voices or voice except by what this person tells you, correct?''

"If they can be heard by other people they are not hallucinations,'' Kelly responded dryly.

Jackson wouldn't be toyed with.''. . . Do you know of any instant in this case where any of the defendant's auditory hallucinations were heard by anyone else?'' she asked sharply.

"No.''

"So, you, basically, you believed what his story was, as far as the auditory hallucinations, and you found him credible, his words, correct?''

"In general, yes,'' Kelly confirmed.

"And you found him to be credible notwithstanding the fact that in 1980 he injected a patient with Xylocaine, came home and lied about having hepatitis, and stayed home for two months, correct?''

"I am aware that he injected with Xylocaine, I'm not aware about the hepatitis story.''

"Were you aware, Doctor Kelly, that in 1984 the defendant had a car accident?''

"Yes.''

''. . . And that he sent a letter to an insurance company as a result of that accident that he simply fell asleep at the wheel of the car; are you aware of that?''

"I was aware of the accident. I wasn't aware of the letter,'' Kelly noted.

Judge Barton felt the need to caution the jurors again. ''The bottom line with all of this, I told you, doesn't come in for the truth of the matters contained therein, it's not evidence of bad character or the propensity to commit crime. The bottom line is how if in any way it affects this Doctor's opinion that he already has given in this particular case.''

Jackson continued moments later, "Doctor Kelly, you're aware, are you not, that this defendant failed to notify hospitals of these episodes while he was in their employ?''

"I think I testified that he did try to cover up his psychotic condition. I don't know the specifics of that vis-a-vis his work in hospitals.''

"Yet you still find him credible?''

"With regard to certain kinds of things, yes, the auditory hallucinations, the psychosis.''

"And you're aware that he lied to his wife and his family, concerning the extent of his illness throughout the years, as well?''

"Yes, I am.''

"And you still find him credible and believable?''

Kelly's certitude seemed to be wearing thin. "About what kinds of things?'' he asked.

"About these auditory hallucinations.''

"Yes, I do.''

"And are you familiar with—you spoke to Doctor Hyndman from California, correct?''

"Yes.''

"Had you seen a letter of September 27, 1990 from Doctor Hyndman?''

"Yes.''

"And are you familiar with Doctor Hyndman stating that the defendant was less than truthful with him, that he only told him what he wanted him to know?''

"I recall that generally in the letter, yes.''

"Yet you still find him credible and believable?''

"Because it's very typical of people with psychotic

conditions to conceal that from family members, psychiatrists, employers, people on the street. That is—I don't attach the significance to that . . . likely to be antisocial personality disorder. Rather, it's a typical kind of thing that someone who is experiencing a psychosis may do both on the way into the floor of a psychosis and on the way out of it to minimize and not fully acknowledge what they are thinking and feeling.''

Jackson looked over at the jury. "So he could have been hiding something from you as well, isn't that correct?''

"That's correct,'' Kelly said.

Jackson established that Kappler had some training in psychiatry and implied that he might have fabricated his symptoms. ". . . Are you familiar . . . with the defendant telling Dr. Kelso to put certain things that he said into the report that he was writing?'' she asked Kelly.

Kelly needed to be directed to the proper page of the report.

"Doctor Kelly,'' Jackson continued, "does that refresh your memory as to whether or not the defendant upon saying certain things to Doctor Kelso suggested that if he reported that to the court it wouldn't hurt his case?''

"That's written in this report, yes,'' Kelly said.

About two hours had passed since Kelly had taken the stand. Jackson was near the end of her questioning. "Are you aware of people, Doctor, who commit senseless acts, who commit murders, who are not insane, and who are able to conform their conduct to the requirements of the law?''

Shapiro objected to the general nature of the question but was overruled by Barton.

"Yes,'' Kelly said.

"And every person that commits a murder, every murder victim doesn't know their perpetrator or their victim, do they?''

''No, they don't,'' Kelly said.

Jackson stood silently for a moment at her desk, nodding. She turned toward John Kappler, then looked back at Kelly. ''Thank you, Doctor,'' she said in dismissal.

# CHAPTER 21

On December 17, Jonathan Shapiro tried to shore up his defense of Kappler by calling to the stand Dr. Ronald Ebert, McLean Hospital's well-respected senior forensic psychologist and a consultant on psychology to the U.S. Congress.

Ebert, near fifty, was bald, wore a moustache and glasses, and dressed in a dark suit and club tie. He had spoken with Kappler for a dozen hours, interviewed Tommie, Jack, and Elsie, and reviewed all Kappler's available medical records. He too was convinced Kappler suffered from a mental disorder and had lost his capacity to abide by the law on April 14, 1990. But he also believed deeply that Kappler couldn't tell right from wrong that day and felt a responsibility to describe for jurors what Kappler had really gone through.

At the start of his testimony, though, he became tangled in psychiatry's nosology. He proposed that Kappler's symptoms best fit with a diagnosis of either atypical psychosis or schizoaffective disorder. "Both are labels that are currently listed in the DSM III-R, the *Diagnostic and Statistical Manual* of the American Psychiatric Association," he explained. "And both are labels that are used for symptoms that don't fit neatly into other more standard categories. But both speak to an illness that is represented by a significant psychotic belief system, delusions and/or hallucinations, and affective—that is, depressive, in this case—symptomatology as well.''

He went on to describe the system of delusions he believed Kappler was consumed by. "It's a system in which he feels like a very small figure. At one point, there is a belief that he's as small as an ant. And it's a system that is very self-deprecating; that he's valueless; that he's no good; that the fact that he's a physician is almost a falsehood, in that he never should have risen to the point that he rose to. It's filled with self-loathing and it's filled with ideas of self-disgust.

"It's a system that has sexual components and homosexual components. It's a system in which there are devils, from time to time. There are ideas of black holes.''

As one of the jurors broke into laughter, Ebert paused, then watched him regain his composure. The expressions of the other jurors told him he was failing to convey any of Kappler's pain.

"All sorts of ideas get blended in," he started again, "but it's a belief system that encompasses all. And other people are involved in it, in fact, everybody knows about it, and his behavior is being watched and there is some test that he has to perform.

"It's also a system in which he needs to be punished. Because he is a worthless and valueless human being, he needs always to suffer in that system and to be punished for his behavior.''

A few jurors looked amused, a few confused, some doubtful.

Ebert felt defeated. "So that's the belief structure," he concluded, "and it's very elaborate and difficult to understand, and obviously not the real world.''

Shapiro seemed to have learned something from Marcy Jackson about bringing in the issue of character. He walked closer to the jury. "And would you tell us what, if anything, you considered significant in the personal history of Dr. Kappler, in terms of your . . . opinion?" he asked.

Ebert reviewed the fact that Kappler had grown up poor, amid physical abuse, that he was embarrassed by having been conceived out of wedlock and felt responsible for his mother. He talked about Kappler's difficult courtship with Tommie and the loss of their child.

But he failed to make a convincing case that the suffering had led to illness, then violence.

One reason he couldn't tell a compelling story about Kappler's life is that he felt he had to avoid talking about those life events that might paint Kappler as an inherently evil person, including his crimes as a boy and young man. But Kappler's rage and lack of feeling for others were at the heart of what was happening to him as a human being. Without those data, the story fell flat.

"The life stresses that I've identified in going through his history, I've highlighted because I think those are stressors that play a significant role in the development of this man's mental illness," he said. "And there are probably others we're not even aware of.

"For me to get a complete picture of anybody and to work with them, I've got to spend a significant amount of time, if I'm going to be treating them, in getting an elaborate history. I have to spend hours and hours to go back and get details, even details people forget because we often forget some of the more stressful details.

"So that in order to come to a detailed understanding, I need a lot of data. And I have collected data, but there's even more that we don't have."

Shapiro took one more step toward the core of his client. "Did you form an opinion, to a reasonable medical certainty," he asked, "as to what, if anything precipitated the episode on April 14th?"

"Yes, I did," Ebert said.

"And what is that opinion?"

". . . I would note that this incident is preceded by a return to the early places where the Kapplers used to live, to people who they used to know in the early days when he was a young medical student and before that.

"And as Dr. Kappler has reported to me, the experience of coming back in a state of a failed reputation, no longer practicing, having been accused of murder, coming back to visit people who are still functioning, still holding their jobs—one of the meetings that the Kapplers went to was an honorary dinner for a physician who Dr. Kappler had worked with in the early days on the East Coast, and the community was coming together to honor this person who had devoted his life and his work to his community.

"And that confrontation between people whose lives were together and successful, and Dr. Kappler coming back, in essence, a ruined person, no longer practicing, no longer able to practice, all sorts of allegations about him; that those were powerful reminders and stresses that I think were precipitous to this illness that resurrected itself, that grew again on the trip back to Boston."

"Can you explain," Shapiro asked, "why . . . stresses which all of us undergo, from time to time, caused in Dr. Kappler something which it doesn't cause in the normal person?"

Ebert didn't venture into psychological theories of how the traumas Kappler experienced as a boy and young man might have laid the groundwork for mental frailty, how being destroyed might lead one to destroy others. It was hard to make that case without suggesting that life events had turned Kappler into a psychopath—a man born decent, then turned bad.

"I certainly do not have a good answer for that," he said. "I don't think the field of . . . psychology or psychiatry has a good answer for that. It may reside in the issue of biology, that some of us are more susceptible than others to mental illness. There are—there is a school of thought that argues strongly for that. . . .

"And certainly, we know that in the case of manic depressive illness, bipolar illness, that that does tend to have some familial origins; that it is unusual for somebody to have a bipolar illness and there not to have been somebody in their family or in the other side of the family with that. So that's a possibility. . . .

"But my experience is, in developing enough of a history, that people who erupt, erupt out of a long history that one can identify and research, given enough time and enough information."

Marcy Jackson wasn't content to question Kappler's character. She knew that jurors would have to trust the medical and psychiatric community—the very people who had seemingly sheltered Kappler during the decades he practiced—in order to declare him insane and release him to their care, so she began her cross-examination of Ebert by immediately casting doubt on his objectivity. ". . . You were hired by the defendant prior to him being brought back to Massachusetts; isn't that correct?" she asked.

"Yes," he said.

"And when were you first contacted, Dr. Ebert?"

"I am not sure I have that information. Let me just check my record and perhaps I—I know I got a phone call from the defendant's attorney prior—I think I have down April 18th and 19th. I believe 18—"

Jackson nodded and glanced over at Kappler. "And he was still in New York at that time; is that correct?"

"Yes, that's correct."

"And individuals from your hospital were contacted even prior to that time; isn't that correct, Doctor?"

"I understand that to be the case, yes."

"In fact . . . prior to him being brought into Payne Whitney, individuals from McLean Hospital were contacted about Dr. Kappler; isn't that correct?"

"I think I know that one individual in particular was, yes."

Jackson established that Ebert was aware of Fred Kelso's report citing the possibility that Kappler had been malingering—inventing symptoms—at Taunton State Hospital. She implied Ebert, already hired by Kappler, might have taken steps to ensure that McLean clinicians would see him as truly sick. "Now, you conferred with your staff prior to Dr. Kappler, the defendant, coming to McLean Hospital; isn't that correct?" she asked.

"I conferred with the Admissions Office, yes," he said. He squinted slightly as if trying to grasp the implication of her question.

"And that was before he was brought in, while he was still at Taunton State Hospital; correct. . . ."

"There were a number of times, so it could have been. . . ."

"And, in fact, you relayed information to McLean's, concerning the defendant's hearing auditory hallucinations and having delusions; did you not, sir?"

"I believe that I did, yes," Ebert said, shrugging, "to the Admissions Office."

"And that was prior to him arriving at your hospital; isn't that correct, sir?"

Ebert agreed.

"And did you, as well, sir, speak with other members

of your hospital about the results of Dr. Kelso's examination, prior to his arriving?''

"Prior to his arriving, I don't believe I did because I don't believe I had seen Dr. Kelso's evaluation by that time," he said.

It was Jackson's tone with Ebert, as much as the very tenuous notion that he had somehow swayed McLean clinicians, that might have moved the jury toward skepticism. With all his expert credentials, Jackson seemed not to trust him. She hammered away again at psychiatry's lack of reliability in diagnosis.

"... He was diagnosed, in 1966, this defendant, as having something different than what he had in '75 and '76; isn't that correct?" she asked.

"Yes," Ebert said. "The diagnoses have varied over time."

Jackson approached the witness stand. "So nobody's really sure of what this defendant suffers from, if he suffers from anything at all?" Jackson asked, stopping and shaking her head.

"Everybody is sure that he suffers from a very serious mental illness . . . ," Ebert protested.

Jackson all but ignored his answer. "Nobody really knows for sure what he suffers from?"

"I know," Ebert said definitively, "that he suffers from a very serious mental illness."

"But we haven't had any consensus among all the experts, sir; have we?"

"We rarely do," Ebert said simply.

Jackson was only getting started. She turned and walked back to her desk. "And isn't it true, though, Doctor, that this defendant gives inconsistent reports about when, exactly, these auditory hallucinations even begin?" she asked.

"Absolutely."

"Doesn't he, in fact, tell you that they didn't occur in 1966?"

"That's right."

"And didn't he then, in fact, tell a member of your staff, upon admission to the hospital, that these auditory hallucinations happened in 1965?"

Ebert had to search the medical record for the admission note.

"... Isn't it true, Doctor, that it states that the defendant, in 1965 at age 35, the patient experienced for the first time auditory hallucinations and developed a paranoid delusional system?" Jackson asked again.

"Yes," Ebert said, "that's what it says here."

"And so, that's inconsistent, sir, with what he told you; is that not correct?"

"That is correct that it is not what he told me."

"And, in fact, sir, on the next page of that admission note, does it not, in fact, state, sir, that the defendant is not sure he had auditory hallucinations in 1980, when he injected a pregnant woman with Xylocaine?"

"Yes."

Jackson went on. "Now, the 1975 incident [on the California freeway], the defendant told you he had auditory hallucinations in 1975; isn't that correct?"

"Yes, that is correct."

"... [But] Mrs. Kappler told Dr. Kelso that ... the auditory hallucinations, were not brought to the Court's attention in 1975; isn't that correct?"

"Yes, I believe that's correct. I remember that."

"... You testified that the defendant, when you discussed the 1985 incident of shutting off the life support system ... didn't state that he was the individual who shut off the life support system—"

"Yes."

"But if you refer to the admission note again, sir, Dr.

Faheda's admission note—and I would direct you to page 3, in the first paragraph . . . does it not state that in 1985, he again experienced some auditory hallucinations and command hallucinations, telling him to unplug the respirator of a quadriplegic person in the anesthesia suite?''

"Yes, that's what it says," Ebert answered, without looking up.

"So he's inconsistent, as well, in whether or not he had auditory hallucinations in 1985?"

Ebert shook his head. What he felt he knew about Kappler—that Kappler's illness was bizarre but very severe—was being effectively buried. "Yes, that's correct."

"But nevertheless, sir, you still believe what he had to say?"

"Yes, I do."

Jackson went over several other inconsistencies in Kappler's reports to various doctors, then moved on to the murky arena of Kappler's capacity on April 14 to abide by the law.

"Now, the defendant is also inconsistent, Dr. Ebert," she began, "with his ability to resist this voice or voices, as he reports; isn't that correct?"

"The resistance is different at different times, yes," Ebert said.

"Well, doesn't he, in fact, tell you that he can initially resist this voice or voices?"

"Yes."

"And doesn't he also indicate that if he heard this voice [tell him] to do a particular thing, that he'd stop and he'd think about whether or not it was a thought boiling up from himself and he'd wait for further instructions?"

Ebert reviewed the medical record, again. "That's what he says, yes," he nodded.

"But nevertheless, sir, you still believe that he's . . . not able to resist these voices?"

"Occasionally, he's not able to, and occasionally, he is."

Jackson shook her head. She looked incredulous. So did the jurors.

"Did he tell you, sir," Jackson asked, "when he's able to resist them and when he's not able to resist them?"

"I don't believe he knows the answer to that," Ebert said.

"Well, do you know the answer, sir?" Jackson asked, her voice slightly raised.

"No, I don't believe I know the answer," Ebert replied, straightening himself in his seat.

"And, in fact, he's been able to resist these voices when they have instructed him to do things such as commit suicide; isn't that correct?"

Ebert disagreed. "There have been times when he has attempted suicide," he said.

Jackson marched through his answer. "However, when it comes time to inject patients with medication or hit them in a car, he cannot resist them; isn't that correct?"

". . . He did not resist them, yes."

"And nevertheless, sir, you still believe him?"

"Yes."

Jackson knew the defense had put forward no compelling psychological explanation for why Kappler would hear voices in the first place. As modern psychiatry does, Shapiro had largely presented his client's symptoms as sterile manifestations of an anonymous illness. Jackson challenged that notion by focusing on Kappler's statement that he couldn't tell whether the voices were connected with his own thoughts.

"Now, isn't it also true, Dr. Ebert," she began, "that the defendant is inconsistent in his representations to various doctors that he's been examined by, as to whether these commands come from these voice or voices, or from within himself?''

"Yes, that's correct."

"And, in fact, he told you, Doctor, that . . . this thing [the idea to drive off the road on April 14] formed in his mind, not in the mind or not as a result of the voice of someone else?''

"Yes."

"And that once it forms in his mind, it was a challenge to him?"

"Yes."

Jackson paused and walked nearer to the jury. "And did he, as well, also tell staff people at McLean Hospital, sir, other than yourself, that he was unable to precisely define these ideas that he—that commanded him to do things?"

"It's my understanding he said that, yes."

"Nevertheless, you believe, sir, that these are voices that command him to do things and he is powerless to resist?"

"I believe that that's his belief, yes."

"And did he not, in fact, tell Dr. Kelso that, at one point, he couldn't recall if the voice or voices were giving him confusing instructions or he'd hear the seed of an idea and he'd enlarge upon it himself?"

"I recall reading that, yes."

"However, it is your opinion that these command hallucinations were directing him to do whatever he did?"

"Yes, I believe that he believed that."

Jackson had Ebert speak about the criteria for a finding of not guilty by reason of insanity, then returned to the issue of character.

"Well, doesn't it matter at all that this defendant had

lied to individuals about his past?'' she asked, her palms upturned in the air.

"Oh yes," Ebert agreed, "it matters."

"And doesn't it matter that he's lied to doctors about information—"

"Absolutely."

"—about his past?"

"Absolutely. It does matter."

"But you, Doctor, were impressed with his sincerity?"

"No, not with his sincerity."

"His honesty?" she said cynically.

"No," Ebert said. "One couldn't argue for his honesty."

"Well, you believed his statements, Doctor; right?"

"Yes. By and large. I mistrusted some and I believed others."

"But it had some impact, his truthfulness, you believed it was there?"

"His presentation was largely believable, yes."

Jackson thanked him and sat down.

Jonathan Shapiro had to repair some of the damage done to the credibility of his expert and to psychiatry as a field. He took the opportunity to redirect questions to Ebert in an effort to dispel some of the doubt Jackson had raised in jurors' minds.

"... Miss Jackson asked you whether or not, on the basis of your review of the medical records in this case, there was disagreement among various experts who had examined Dr. Kappler. Did you take into account these various opinions?" he asked.

"Yes, I did," Ebert said confidently.

"And ... what significance, if any, did you attribute to the differences in the diagnoses?"

Ebert took a deep breath, no doubt grateful for another

chance to explain. "The significance I attributed to the difference in the diagnoses was that this clearly was an illness difficult to diagnose for most experienced clinicians; that the symptoms were of a variety, that covered a variety of different illnesses; and that people were having a hard time arriving at a single cubby hole, if you will, to stick Dr. Kappler in. There was no disagreement, in my reading of any of the medical records, with the opinion that he suffers from a very serious mental illness. That was consistent across every hospitalization he's ever had.''

Shapiro nodded tentatively. He was still hearing that his client didn't fit any standard diagnosis. "And with respect to the nature of this serious mental illness," he went on, "was there any disagreement as to whether or not the mental illness was a psychotic mental illness?"

"I don't recall any disagreement with that."

"Now Miss Jackson asked you about various inconsistencies in the reports that Dr. Kappler has given you, with respect to the events of April 14th. Did you consider these inconsistencies?"

"Well, I have reviewed them in some detail," Ebert said. "First of all, many of the inconsistencies are on rather minor points of was it one voice or three voices, was there a voice at this moment as opposed to that moment. My understanding of the psychotic experience— and I have worked with many people who have experienced this—is that it is a confusing, disorganizing and terrifying experience.

"And when one asks somebody a week later, a month later, a day later to report their experience, they often have a very difficult time. They have a difficult time because their thought process was confused at the moment and they are trying to make sense of it afterwards.

"Some of Dr. Kappler's statements to me and to others,

'Well, maybe it was a thought, rather than a voice,' is, in my opinion, an attempt to understand what was going on when one didn't understand what was going on. It's an attempt to make sense of something that doesn't feel sensible.''

Shapiro now confronted the character issue directly. ''And would you explain to the jury why you believed that Dr. Kappler was attempting to be honest and candid with you?''

Ebert seemed glad for the opportunity. ''I'm very familiar with the literature on malingering,'' he said, ''and very familiar with the data that we've attempted to collect in the mental health field, to see if what people tell us is accurate or not.

''It's hard to know because people are reporting their own words. I mean I can't read anybody's mind. I am not able to read what somebody is thinking. I have to get that information by asking them.

''And so, I make that assessment every time I sit with somebody. I make the assessment every time I sit with family members.

''And in my opinion, sitting with this man, over a period of—I don't know, eight interviews or a dozen interviews, however many it was—in my assessment of the pain that I saw and the anguish, and in my assessment of what he was withholding—not only with what he was telling, but what he wasn't telling me—I saw somebody who was minimizing, avoiding, not telling me things that would have been dramatic examples of his illness. He wasn't overwhelming me with information and he wasn't trying to persuade me that . . . [he was] crazy as a March hare.

''In fact, he was—he spent most of [his] time or much of his time, I should say, trying to persuade me that [he] was a good father, that he was a fine physician and that when he wasn't crazy, that he tried to provide care and good health to people.

"He was attempting to persuade me that he wasn't as bad, as evil or as malicious as his behaviors looked like.

"I weighed that. I weighed the way in which he provided me with information. . . .

"And it was my sense, on many occasions, that he was lying to me and trying to persuade me, and himself I suspect, that everything was fine. Which, of course, is what I think has gone on for too long in his illness over the years. And he has occasionally persuaded people of that.

"So I attempted to be skeptical. Despite my skepticism, with my experience and with my many hours of interviewing him, I came to the conclusion that, by and large, the things that he was telling me were things that he genuinely believed and were accurate reports of what he felt his mental state to be at the time."

Marcy Jackson had only one question for her "recross" examination:

". . . A major mental illness doesn't necessarily mean that the defendant is unable to appreciate the wrongfulness of his conduct or conform his conduct to the requirements of law; does it, Doctor?"

"No, it does not," Ebert said evenly.

Dr. Robert Aranow, Kappler's attending psychiatrist during the four months he was an inpatient at McLean Hospital, also testified on December 17. He had visited with Kappler at least forty-five times during his hospital stay.

Aranow had been educated at Harvard and Columbia and had been a consultant to the American Psychiatric Association on the development of the DSM III-R. But even he, when asked by Shapiro to comment on Kappler's diagnosis, couldn't speak about the book without spotlighting its ambiguities.

"Will you describe what, in your opinion, is the mental disease from which Dr. Kappler is suffering?" Shapiro directed him.

"The technical diagnosis that I came upon," Aranow began, "was psychotic disorder not otherwise specified, which is otherwise called 'atypical psychosis.' . . ."

Shapiro asked if that diagnosis was one that seemed to fit Kappler's symptoms from the beginning to the end of his stay on Aranow's ward.

Aranow nodded confidently, but his answer was anything but reassuring to jurors. "The diagnosis 'atypical psychosis' is a diagnosis you reach once you've looked at other possible diagnoses . . . and if they don't fit, you wind up saying they're psychotic but it doesn't fit these other diagnoses."

"So, I didn't have an initial diagnosis [when first hearing of Kappler], except that he probably needed to be in a psychotic unit, since I hadn't met him yet. . . ."

Marcy Jackson's appetite for documenting psychiatry's imperfect diagnostic scheme was insatiable. "Your experience of this psychosis is somewhat unusual?" she asked Aranow.

"Extremely," he allowed.

"No one can really put their finger on it?"

Aranow may have seen that he was about to be cornered and attempted to sidestep. "I'm not sure what you mean by 'put your finger on it.' "

"Well, no one can really define what mental disease or defect this defendant is suffering from?"

"Well," Aranow hedged, "I don't want to—mental illnesses are categorized by looking at a lot of other mental illnesses, and most of them fall in sort of categories but they vary within those categories. And this illness does not fall into any one of those simple categories, as many do not fall into those categories.'' He paused and seemed to review mentally what he had said, to make sure it made sense. ''Dr. Kappler's is, unfortunately,'' he went on, ''an extremely unusual form of psychosis.''

For the next two days the jury heard from forensic psychologists Tyler Carpenter and Fred Kelso. Neither was willing to state definitively that Kappler was in control of his behavior on April 14—and neither was willing to exclude the possibility that he suffered from a psychotic illness. But each included in his testimony the possibility that Kappler's was primarily or purely a problem of character, that he was an antisocial and narcissistic man—a destructive person, a psychopath—who heard his own detached rageful and violent thoughts echoing in his mind the day Paul Mendelsohn died and Deborah Brunet-Tuttle was so severely injured. Both noted that Kappler seemed to exercise discretion in obeying some ''voices'' and not others. And both wondered aloud whether at least some of the psychiatric signs and symptoms Kappler demonstrated or complained of to them, including his requests for oral sex, might have been fabricated to enhance his chances of acquittal.

# CHAPTER 22

With all the experts having weighed in, the bulk of them solidly on his side, Jonathan Shapiro delivered a fifty-minute closing argument, sometimes rambling, sometimes impassioned, on December 21.

He began by walking slowly over to the jury and looking into one pair of eyes after another. "First of all, I want to thank you on behalf of my client and myself for your attention and patience throughout this long and at times, I'm sure, tedious trial," he started off.

"As I said in my opening statement, the death of Paul Mendelsohn and the injuries to Ms. Brunet-Tuttle were a terrible, terrible tragedy to all concerned. You probably have heard enough about Dr. Kappler in the course of this trial to know the remorse and the anguish and the guilt that he has suffered and will always suffer.

"You've heard testimony about it, and I think you've seen it on his face during the trial.

"This is something which you know, I'm sure, that if being found guilty of the crime of murder could bring back Paul Mendelsohn or restore Ms. Tuttle to health, Dr. Kappler would be the first one to say, 'Find me guilty.' "

Shapiro looked over at his client, whose face was expressionless, then turned back to the jury. "But, unfortunately, ladies and gentlemen," he said, shaking his head, "that's not possible. And it's your duty today to decide, solely on the basis of the law and evidence whether Dr. Kappler is to be branded a murderer or whether he is to be recognized as a mentally ill person who suffers, and has suffered all his life from a cruel and terrifying disease, which has in a very real way, destroyed his life in a way that is hard to imagine.

"I said in my opening statement, and I'm saying now that Dr. Kappler admits that he killed Paul Mendelsohn, and that he injured Ms. Tuttle. That is not the issue in this case at all, and because of that, you need not waste your time going through thirty-eight photographs, pieces of evidence, exhibits to establish what the car looked like, where it was located, who found it, the various exhibits which the Commonwealth has introduced in the course of its case, because that really is not an issue in the case.

"Rather, the only issue in the case is why it happened.

"Did it happen, as Ms. Jackson will argue, because Dr. Kappler is a cold blooded murderer who intended to kill or maim? Is it, as Ms. Jackson will argue, because as a child Dr. Kappler developed a personality defect because his father forced him to fight local bullies who chased him, to fight them against his will?

"Is it a personality defect that developed because he stole bottles for their deposit, threw tomatoes at some people in a bar, or, once at the age of fifteen stole a car with some friends and wrecked it?

"Or, as I suggest, did it happen because Dr. Kappler, throughout his life, has suffered from a debilitating mental illness which on occasion transformed him from a solid citizen, a reputable doctor, a good husband and father, into a deranged and sometimes violent person?

"Did it happen because, as has happened other times in his life, on April 14, 1990, he found himself in the grips of a psychosis which caused him to enter a nightmarish world—a nightmarish world of delusions and hallucinations, a world where he lost completely, any contact with the reality that you or I know, and was governed by a strange and irresistible power?"

Shapiro highlighted the fact that every expert witness had listed the diagnosis of atypical psychosis after assessing Kappler. "It is a disease," he went on, "which is always there, but because of, perhaps, biological factors, perhaps because of stressors in his life, from time to time, inexplicably erupts like a volcano, transforming him into a different person."

He ran through Kappler's psychiatric hospitalizations over the course of three decades and leaned close to the jurors. "The only way to explain what happened on April 14 is that this was the reappearance of the disease from which he has suffered and had affected his life so many times in the past, and this was the same disease that the experts who examined him after that date determined he was, and, is suffering from throughout his life.

"The only real issue, therefore, comes down to whether or not the Commonwealth [of Massachusetts] has met its burden of proving beyond a reasonable doubt that on April 14, as a result of this serious mental disease, Dr. Kappler nevertheless possessed substantial capacity to appreciate the wrongfulness of his conduct and, that despite this disease, on April 14 he possessed the substantial capacity to conform his conduct to the requirements of the law.

"That is the Commonwealth's burden, and it's up to the Commonwealth to prove both of those things to you beyond a reasonable doubt.

"And ladies and gentlemen, I submit to you that the

Commonwealth has not even come close to meeting that very heavy burden of proof. . . .

" . . . The Commonwealth has not presented a single witness who is willing or able to venture an expert opinion that on April 14, 1990, Dr. Kappler was sane, was legally sane, was able to understand, able to conform his conduct to the law."

Jurors in Massachusetts have the right to disregard all expert testimony and judge the defendant's sanity for themselves, but Shapiro hoped they would rely on the experts.

"As the Judge has instructed you throughout the trial, you can believe or disbelieve the testimony of any expert, and the decision, the ultimate decision, is yours.

"But, ladies and gentlemen, the reason that the law recognizes expert testimony, and permits experts to testify in a trial such as this, is that it recognizes that experts, on the basis of their experience, their training, their background, their expertise, are able to contribute opinions, information, which can assist you, the jury, in resolving the issue which is beyond the understanding of most people.

"The issue in this case is a question, a difficult question, of criminal responsibility based upon the determination of psychiatric evidence, psychological considerations which some people are trained in, and have spent their life developing an expertise.

"And, that is why the law recognizes that those people can come and testify, and give an opinion in a case like that.

"And I suggest to you that the failure of the Commonwealth to present a single witness who can contribute that opinion to you is enough, in and of itself, to indicate that it has failed to meet its burden of proof.

"It is the Commonwealth's responsibility to present

evidence to you, upon which you can then feel comfortable in making a decision concerning something of this magnitude.

"And, when the Commonwealth has not been able to present that evidence, I submit to you that it is unfair to ask you to do its job and fill its gaps for it."

After reviewing some of Kappler's symptoms on his trip to Boston, Shapiro focused on the morning of April 14. "When he got into the car, and perhaps the only picture which is of any relevance is the photograph of the interior of the car which shows the three Snicker bars in the well in the front seat. And, those Snicker bars conveyed the message to Dr. Kappler that his wife, his daughter and Alex were snickering at him, laughing at him; and 'Snick' became 'Nick,' and to him that was the devil.

"Now, this doesn't make any sense," Shapiro went on, "but it indicates the extent to which his mind, by that time, was deranged, and that he was, at this time, engrossed in the delusions that he was suffering . . . [and] he began to hear the auditory hallucinations, the voice that would direct him to leave the apartment, to drive down Alewife Brook Parkway, to leave the Parkway onto the footpath, to hit Paul Mendelsohn and Ms. Tuttle, and leave the area, wander around, and go to New York.

"Isn't it clear that . . . [as] Ms. Kappler testified, Dr. Kappler abruptly left the apartment that morning without finishing his breakfast, seeming abrupt to her at the time? She didn't attach the kind of significance she wishes she had, but he left abruptly.

"Isn't it clear that he was already in the grips of this powerful force? Isn't it clear that when, moments before, he left the apartment, he drove through the red light, gripping the wheel, intensely concentrating on focusing, that at that time he was in the grips of something which was controlling him?'' Shapiro paused and spread his palms in the air. ''. . . Because, otherwise, why at that time, would he have driven through a red light?

''Is this the result of a personality defect? Is this because he has an antisocial personality which causes him to [dis]obey traffic laws?

''No, I suggest to you that that is an indication that as of that time, sometime even before he reached the scene of the accident, that he was already in the grips of the voice that was directing him what to do and how to do it.''

Shapiro may have read cynicism on one of the jurors' faces. ''Ladies and gentlemen,'' he beseeched the jury, ''the only explanation for that kind of conduct is insanity. There was no reason for what he did. There was no purpose. And, there was no conceivable gain to him to do what he did.

''In fact, the opposite was true. He had everything to lose, his good name, his family, his liberty. Everything was something that he had to lose by virtue of what he did, similar to what had happened in the past when he had done equally bizarre irrational acts where there was no gain, and only loss. In 1975, in 1980, in 1985. All of these things reflected the diseased mind that was compelled to do things that were aganist any conceivable interest he could ever have, or that of his family.''

Shapiro turned and gestured toward Marcy Jackson. ''On the basis of the examination of the witnesses,'' he said, ''I suggest that Ms. Jackson will probably argue that this is all made up. That Dr. Kappler is feigning mental illness, and has for the past twenty-five years, for one reason or another, feigned the illness, deceived the physicians who were treating him, and done that, presumably, to some purpose about which there is, certainly, no evidence in this case.

"I suggest to you that it is extremely improbable that Dr. Kappler would have been able to deceive every expert who has come in here and testified concerning what happened. . . .

". . . When Dr. Kappler said to Dr. Kelso, and some of the other experts, 'I think it was my own voice,' well, of course it was his own voice; and, now, when he has come out of the psychosis, he realizes it was his own voice. It wasn't a real voice telling him to do this. It was his own voice. Not a voice, as you and I might talk to ourselves to remind us to do an errand, or say, 'Let's not forget to do this or that.'

"No. The voice was Dr. Kappler's voice, but it was a voice—his own voice transformed by an illness into a psychotic powerful force that was controlling his conduct, and over which he was powerless to resist.

"Yes, it is his voice, but it was the voice of an illness, of a psychosis speaking to him from a nightmare world where he had been transformed.

"Dr. Kappler hasn't tried to deceive physicians who examined him. He hasn't tried to make up symptoms. In fact, all the witnesses have said the opposite is true. He denied hallucinations. He's denied delusions when, if you were trying to put one over on somebody, it would be the easiest thing in the world to say, 'I'm still hearing the voice, and the voice is making me do this or that. . . .'

". . . Ms. Jackson may also suggest the fact that Dr. Kappler left the scene was indicative that he knew that what he had done was wrong.

"Well, I suggest to you ladies and gentlemen, that that does not indicate that at all.

"Rather, what Dr. Kappler did was more consistent with somebody acting in the throes of a psychosis. . . . If he had been attempting to escape, why would he have left his badly damaged car in the driveway of somebody's house, full of identification, where it could clearly be discovered almost immediately?

"Why, if he were trying to escape, would he have walked past the scene of the accident, where he risked being recognized by any one of the witnesses who might have seen him drive by?

"Why, if he were trying to escape, did he go to New York and wander throughout the city for an entire day before calling his wife, going to a psychiatric clinic, and making his whereabouts known to the authorities?

"I suggest to you that none of this in any way indicates that he knew what he was doing was wrong. Rather, what he was doing was what the voice was directing him to do, the same overwhelmingly powerful compulsion that had existed throughout the day, and would continue throughout the next day."

Shapiro next challenged what he predicted would be Jackson's contention that Kappler had the capacity to pick and choose which commands to obey. He cited the fact that Kappler had crashed his own car more than once and had been hospitalized in the intensive care unit on one occasion. . . . "Everything that he has ever done when in the throes of a psychotic episode," he asserted, "everything he's ever done has been self-destructive. It ran counter to everything he lives for and believes in when he is not in a psychotic state. It ran counter to his reputation, to his family, to his life, and to all of the interest which he held dear.

"Nothing he did ever advanced himself or any conceivable interest that he may have had.

"Ladies and gentlemen, in the face of the overwhelming expert and other evidence that Dr. Kappler was, on April 14, 1990, completely and utterly unable to appreciate the wrongfulness of his conduct or to conform it to the law [t]he arguments of the Commonwealth do not even approach meeting its burden of proving guilt and sanity beyond a reasonable doubt.

"And I am confident that you will, because of that, return a verdict of not guilty by reason of insanity."

Shapiro ended by reading a portion of the *Los Angeles Times* op-ed piece Kappler had written under a pseudonym. " 'No. I didn't laugh at the crazy man on the bus,' " Shapiro read quietly. " 'Instead, I eased up on him ever so gently, entering his territory ever so gingerly. I didn't touch him. Speaking softly, I told him that he needed a friend. I told him I was concerned for him. That I was afraid that he'd be hurt or would hurt somebody else. I told him that he needed a doctor. He needed to be admitted to a hospital. I mentioned both County Hospital and Camarillo. But then, after giving him the dollar he'd asked for, I got off at my stop. I pray to God that he found his.' "

Shapiro nodded slowly, then looked from juror to juror. "Ladies and gentlemen," he concluded, his voice full of emotion, "you the jury are Dr. Kappler's last stop after a long and troubled life. And I pray to God that, consistent with the law and the evidence in this case, that you show him the same understanding and consideration that he showed to the poor man on the bus.

"Thank you."

Marcy Jackson stood to deliver her closing argument after a five-minute recess. She looked back at Deborah Brunet-Tuttle seated in her wheelchair and at the family of Paul Mendelsohn in the first row of spectators. Then she approached the jury.

"May it please the Court, Mr. Shapiro, ladies and gentlemen of the jury . . . I would agree with Mr. Shapiro insofar as there are two positions in this case," she began. "The Commonwealth's position, ladies and gentlemen, is that this defendant, on April 14, 1990, intentionally drove off onto the running path on the Alewife Brook Parkway and intentionally hit Paul Mendelsohn, thereby killing him; and intentionally hit Deborah Brunet-Tuttle, and that he was criminally responsible for his actions on that day.''

She turned and looked briefly at Kappler. ''The defendant's position, ladies and gentlemen, is that although he did these things, he's not criminally responsible.

''Take a look at these two theories, ladies and gentlemen, these two positions, and see what they're grounded in. See what forms the basis of both these positions.

''The Commonwealth's position . . . is based on facts, facts that you know, facts that are in evidence, facts and the reasonable inferences that you can draw from those facts.

''The defendant's position is based on opinion. Opinion of individuals who weren't there on April 14th of 1990. Opinions of individuals who weren't there in 1966, 1975, 1976, 1980, 1981, 1984 or 1985. Opinions of individuals who can't look into this defendant's mind and read it. Opinions of individuals who can't hear these hallucinations and verify that they exist. That's what the defendant's case is based on, those opinions.

''What facts? What facts do you know, ladies and gentlemen? You know that on April 14, 1990 this defendant got up, got dressed, and he appeared fine to his family. He had breakfast. He neatly packed his car. He got directions to New York, made a phone call, said his goodbyes, and was on his way.

''You know for a fact, ladies and gentlemen, that he made his way down to the Alewife Brook Parkway in Somerville, and that he continued to drive down the Alewife Brook Parkway, and after he passed Broadway on the Alewife Brook Parkway, he was driving his car in a controlled manner, staying on the right-hand side of the road.

"And you know for a fact, ladies and gentlemen, that as he continued towards Henderson Street on the Alewife Brook Parkway he slowly started to bring his car over to the right. And you know for a fact, ladies and gentlemen, that after the Henderson Street Bridge, this defendant mounted the curb onto that running path. You know for a fact that not before, during or after he got onto this running path did he attempt to swerve, did he stop, did he sound his horn, did he brake.

". . . You know for a fact that his car was found within minutes of the incident, and it was found off a side street, tucked into a back—a driveway or an area out of sight. You know for a fact that the defendant wasn't in that car at the time it was found. . . .

". . . You know for a fact that he ended up in New York the next day, and that he called his daughter. . . .

"And you also know, ladies and gentlemen, that the police were not told that he contacted the family during that period of time. And you also know, ladies and gentlemen, that he wasn't found in the same clothing that the police originally [were] told he was wearing when he left the house on April 14, 1990, and that clothing having no evidentiary value to it whatsoever.

"You know for a fact, ladies and gentlemen, that he checked into the Payne Whitney Clinic on April 15th of 1990 when the police were looking for him."

She pointed to Kappler. "And you know for a fact that this defendant stands before you accused of murder, accused of assault with intent to murder.

"And what about these [expert] opinions?" Jackson said, shaking her head as if in disbelief and starting to pace. "Again, they're opinions of individuals who weren't there on April 14th, who can't look into his mind.

Opinions of individuals who were relying on what this defendant tells them.''

She stopped and dropped her voice to a grave tone. ''You also have observations of individuals, ladies and gentlemen, observations of people who have been trying to cover up for what this defendant has been doing for the past fifteen years. You have observations of people who understandably have been trying to rationalize what this defendant has been doing. You have observations of people who—who, it is reasonable to assume, have a difficult time accepting certain facts.

''You have observations of individuals, ladies and gentlemen, who for the past fifteen years, have been trying to protect only one person. That's the defendant.

''These opinions, ladies and gentlemen, you are obligated to listen to them, but you are not required to accept them. They are opinions, ladies and gentlemen, of individuals the defendant hired. Hired before he even went into the Payne Whitney Clinic. . . .

''. . . Separate fact from opinion, and then use your common sense. Because if any case cries out for common sense, then this is the one because, ladies and gentlemen, keep in mind that actions speak louder than words.''

She motioned over at Kappler again. ''Now, is this defendant—does he have a mental disease or defect? Well, the Commonwealth will concede to you, ladies and gentlemen, that this defendant has problems, so does any individual who commits a senseless act like this. No question about it. But does that mean that this defendant is not criminally responsible? He can be psychotic and criminally responsible. It's up to you to decide.

''And these experts have told you that this is a mental disease or defect. Well, what about this disease or defect? What do we know about [it]? It's called 'atypical.' What does that mean? It means no one can figure it out.

"That means that this defendant has been given diagnosis after diagnosis over the years, and they put it in a category and they call it, 'not otherwise defined,' because the bottom line is they can't define it. . . .

". . . The only time this psychosis is apparent is when this defendant goes to the hospital where his experts are employed. That's when they look for things. That's when they talk about it. That's when they say, 'Look out for this suspicious behavior.'

"And what else is unusual about this illness? It has a remarkable—a remarkable resemblance to a simple personality disorder, for someone who has had this throughout his life. A personality disorder, antisocial behavior, an individual who enjoys the exploits of criminals.

"What else is unusual about the illness, ladies and gentlemen? What about these voices? The defendant reports one voice, two voices, multiple voices. He reports the voice of God, the devil or some woman he knew. What about those voices? And, are they voices?

"The defendant even says, and Dr. Kelso questions that, whether there are voices or they're just ideas." Jackson shook her head cynically. "These aren't voices, ladies and gentlemen. These are ideas that all of us may, at one time or another, entertain. But this defendant is different because he acts upon his ideas."

Jackson cast doubt on the severity of Kappler's symptoms by highlighting that he seemed able to resist commands to kill himself, that he generally reported his symptoms only once he had run afoul of the law, and that he was often able to avoid hospitalization.

"Was he being hospitalized in 1980 during the incident with the pregnant woman and the Xylocaine?" she asked. "Was he being hospitalized in 1984 when he committed similar mischief with a patient? No. Was he hospitalized in 1985 when a respirator was shut off? No. . . .

". . . And every time, ladies and gentlemen, every time, with the expressed consent of . . . this Dr. Hyndman—he sends him back to work. He's fine. Clean bill of health. Four days in the hospital, and he can go back to that hospital anesthetizing individuals.

"What does that tell you about the treatment of this illness, whether there even is an illness?

"What about the defendant's own accounts of this illness. He inconsistently tells different people, depending on who he talks to. He tries to hide things. He tries to misrepresent them. You know he's lied about things in the past. You know he's misrepresented things in the past, and I suggest to you, he has a motive to do so again today.

"And, importantly, ladies and gentlemen, think about how this defendant even considers his own illness, whether he considers himself to be ill. He goes back each and every time, with such insight into his dangerousness, with such insight into the unpredictability . . . goes back each and every time, into the workplace. A doctor. Into the workplace.

". . . Just think about it. Mr. Shapiro has talked about this senseless act, and [how] there's no . . . [rationale] for it. That a doctor, someone who has been trained to sustain life, to protect life, would actually go out there and do something like that. 'Well, gee. He must be crazy.'

"Well, think about it, ladies and gentlemen. The same doctor who has been trained the same way to sustain and protect life, after he knows the extent of his illness. . . . Every time he goes back. He goes back to work and he subjects more people to that.

"What does that tell you about how serious he considers his illness?

"The defendant writes about his illness. Well, ladies and gentlemen, his insights into his illness are just words, basically. It might sell newspapers, but you don't have to buy it here.''

Jackson looked angry. She paused to collect herself, then continued. "I suggest one thing to you. I suggest you look at it in terms of whether this defendant was able to understand what he was doing, whether he was able to understand whether it was wrong.

"His own expert, Dr. Kelly, even admits he thinks the defendant, in his opinion, could appreciate the wrongfulness of his conduct.

"Do you think he could appreciate the wrongfulness of his conduct, ladies and gentlemen? Do you think he could appreciate the wrongfulness of his conduct before he left that house where he saw these signposts, heard these voices, but he chose to get into that car, and continued driving and not tell anyone? Do you think he appreciated the wrongfulness of his conduct, ladies and gentlemen, when he waited until he reached a stretch in that road which didn't have any houses, and he went off the road into a deserted area?

"Do you think he appreciated the wrongfulness of his conduct . . . when he hit Paul Mendelsohn on the right-hand side of his car and kept going and left him there? Do you think he could have appreciated the wrongfulness of his conduct?

"And these words, 'hit and run,' by themselves, ladies and gentlemen, suggest that someone can appreciate the wrongfulness of their conduct. Hit and then run.''

She looked over at Kappler with disgust. "And he ended up in New York. He didn't stay in Massachusetts. He fled the jurisdiction. Why? Because he could appreciate the wrongfulness of his conduct.

"And, he contacted a doctor and he got checked into a hospital before anybody else was notified. Why is that?

Because he could appreciate the wrongfulness of his conduct.

"Facts, ladies and gentlemen. Facts that you have. Facts that you know versus words that this defendant has told his experts.

". . . And what about this defendant's ability to conform his conduct to the requirements of the law? Again, the Commonwealth has the burden to prove beyond a reasonable doubt that this defendant had the substantial capacity to conform his conduct to the requirements of law.

"And again, ladies and gentlemen, I suggest to you that the Commonwealth has met its burden. The facts versus the opinions. The facts versus this defendant's statement.

"How do you define that [capacity], ladies and gentlemen? Again, Justice Barton will give you instructions on what that term means. But let me suggest that you look at [it] . . . exactly how this defendant's experts have. . . . As 'choices.' As a 'capacity to choose.' Capacity to choose in self-interest.

"When it came time to obeying voices, to run down two people on a running path, this defendant was powerless," Jackson said sarcastically. "He was unable to choose. But when it came time to protect himself, self-protection, self-serving, this defendant found it real easy to resist those voices, real easy to choose.

"How do you know he had the capacity to conform his conduct to the requirements of the law? Because he chose how to implement this crime. He chose that area. He chose how to hit Paul Mendelsohn, how to hit Deborah Brunet-Tuttle with the right-hand side of his car. Not straight ahead, not into his line of vision. He protected himself. He made that choice, and he continued to go down that path, continued to leave that scene because he made the choice, that self-protection, to get out of there. He had the capacity to choose.

"And choosing to go around that corner, out of sight, off the route of travel he was taking . . . he had the capacity to make that decision, and he chose it. And he chose to park his car down at the end of that alley, tucked away into that driveway so no one could see it from the street. Because, ladies and gentlemen, it was another decision that this defendant made in his self-interest.

"His words, ladies and gentlemen, versus the facts you know. When it came time to throw himself in front of the cars on [Route] 95. . . . He didn't do it. These voices, as he tells you, let him off the hook.

"What about in New York when he told people that he was following commands to kill himself? . . . He chose otherwise.

"What does it tell you about his ability to conform his conduct? When it comes time to kill any other people, he can't conform. When it comes time for self-preservation and protection, it's easy to disobey."

Jackson stared intently at the jurors. "Ladies and gentlemen," she said quietly,. "is this behavior intentional behavior? Yes. Is it senseless behavior? No question about it. Is it criminal behavior? Yes. . . . No doubt about it.

"The real tragedy in this case, ladies and gentlemen, is this had gone on for too long. Modern psychology, that's what the defendant wants you to believe. Do you really want to believe in it in this case, ladies and gentlemen? Do you really want to put your faith in what this defendant has told his experts and what they're trying— what they're trying to sell you?

"Do you want to believe it in this case? I suggest not. Are you required to believe it in this case? Not at all. Do you need to believe it in this case? Absolutely not.

"Actions speak louder than words."

# CHAPTER 23

When you stand before me and look at me, what do you
know of the pains that are in me, and what do I know of
yours? And if I were to prostrate myself before you, and
weep and talk, would you know any more about me than
you know about Hell when someone tells you that it is hot
and fearsome?

—Franz Kafka

On December 21, 1990, Judge Robert Barton gave the
jury its charge, including the direction that they were not
bound to decide the defendant's guilt or innocence based
on expert testimony. "You should consider their testimony," he said, "in connection with the other evidence
in this case, and give it such weight as, in your judgement,
it is fairly entitled to receive."

He then cautioned them that Kappler's behavior in
years prior to the crime should not alter their judgment
of him. "A person is insane, and, therefore, not criminally
responsible for his actions," he said, "if, at the time of
those acts, he suffered from a mental disease or defect,
and as a result of that mental disease or defect, he either
lacks substantial capacity to appreciate the criminality, the
wrongfulness of his conduct, or he lacks the substantial
capacity to conform his conduct to the requirements of
the law."

The jury was led out of the courtroom to deliberate.
Just two hours later, they notified the clerk that they had
come to a decision on each of the charges. It seemed that

either the defense or the prosecution had utterly failed to make its case.

Before the jury returned to the courtroom, Judge Barton urged the spectators to stay in control when the verdicts were announced: "This has been an emotional case, and I'm sure that most of you are emotionally involved. Now, please, try your very best to control your emotions, because we have to go through some legal procedures in order to receive the verdicts and whatever. So, please try your very best to keep yourself under control."

The jury filed in.

Jonathan Shapiro and John Kappler stood together to receive the verdict.

"Mr. Foreman," Judge Barton asked, "has your jury agreed upon its verdicts?"

"Yes, we have," the foreman answered.

The clerk read each charge. "As to Indictment 90–1762, this indictment charging murder in the second degree, what say you, Mr. Foreman, is the defendant guilty or not guilty?"

"Guilty of murder in the second degree."

"As to Indictment 90–1763, this indictment charging armed assault with intent to murder, what say you, Mr. Foreman, is the defendant guilty or not guilty?"

"Guilty of armed assault with intent to murder."

"Indictment 90–1764, this indictment charging assault and battery by means of a dangerous weapon, what say you, Mr. Foreman, is the defendant guilty or not guilty?"

"Guilty."

Jonathan Shapiro immediately requested that his client be confined at Metropolitan State Hospital, but Judge Barton reminded him that Kappler was now the responsibility of the Department of Corrections rather than the Department of Mental Health.

And with that, Dr. John Frederick Kappler, Jr., who

had seen his acceptance to medical school as a cancellation of his tortured past, was given the mandatory sentence of life imprisonment, to be served at the Massachusetts Correctional Institute at Cedar Junction.

Three years later, on December 15, 1993, the Supreme Judicial Court of Massachusetts rejected his appeal for a new trial.

"I hope he never gets out," a relative of Kappler who wished to remain anonymous said. "He could walk out and look normal, but it could happen again. Believe me."

Alexander Solzhenitsyn wrote, "If only it were all so simple! If only there were evil people somewhere committing evil deeds, and it were necessary only to separate them from the rest of us and destroy them. But the line dividing good and evil cuts through the heart of every human being. And who is willing to destroy a piece of his own heart?"

By the time John Kappler's case came to an end, twelve citizen jurors and a prosecutor, with the support of two Massachusetts courts, had concluded he was guilty of ending Paul Mendelsohn's life and attempting to end Deborah Brunet-Tuttle's. They judged that he had knowingly embarked on a path of destructiveness and was responsible for horrifying violence. They had decided to punish him and, perhaps, deter others from similar acts by sending him to prison for the rest of his life.

The core rationale for their judgments was embodied in a central question Marcy Jackson had put to Dr. Martin Kelly. "Are you aware of people, Doctor," she had asked, "who commit senseless acts, who commit murders, who are not insane, and who are able to conform their conduct to the requirements of the law?"

Kelly had answered in the affirmative, agreeing that

people sometimes make conscious and rational decisions to hurt or kill people they have never met.

Modern psychiatry stands with him. By means of a cookbook diagnostic manual, some people are diagnosed with major mental illnesses like schizophrenia or bipolar disorder that can so distort their ability to think and to perceive the world around them that they are occasionally absolved of responsibility for violence. Other people who have no regard for the truth and no regard for human life—those the nineteenth-century physician John Pritchard described as morally insane—are almost always considered to have chosen to commit dark deeds freely.

But what if our notions about free choice, destructiveness, and illness have failed us? What if people born good can be harmed in such a way that their innate capacity for human relatedness—for empathy—is broken or shattered? What if their insanity, their disease, is the compulsion to create in the world some physical representation of the hopelessness, callousness, and suffering they themselves endured? What if leaving Paul Mendelsohn and Deborah Brunet-Tuttle as anonymous victims chosen at random was an uncontrollable expression of John Kappler's frustration, pain, and rage at having been born by chance into a kind of hell?

Many of us know in our hearts that this can occur. When a man walks into a restaurant and opens fire or a teenager kills another teenager for sport, no inanimate, anonymous demon is asserting itself. A life under pressure has boiled over. Natural human sensitivities have been perverted, turned rancid, and then turned inside out.

There is terrible tragedy when a person's inborn capacity for humanity is twisted, but our legal system turns us away from that suffering and focuses us narrowly on assessing blame and doling out punishment. In so doing, it allows us to pretend that our own sensitivities are incorruptible, that we are wholly different from the assailants and killers among us. This dangerous myth blinds us to our own suffering and our own potential for destructiveness and denies us a greater empathic understanding of others. We risk becoming like the victimizer to the extent we fail to see that person as a victim.

Psychiatry increasingly sanctions this illusory chasm between them and us by medicalizing and empiricizing, and in the process sterilizing, the range of human emotional experience. A field that could be an increasingly bright light in exploring dark regions of the psyche has come to settle for labels like "intermittent explosive disorder" and "personality disorder not otherwise specified."

This artificial chasm cuts off creative solutions to the epidemic of violence our society now faces. There was, after all, nothing else to be done with a man as dangerous as John Kappler other than locking him away in a prison for life. Our mental health system is shoddy, underfunded, and unreliable in dealing with violent offenders. The resources devoted to mental health research, particularly in the area of violence prevention, are so paltry as to be a national embarrassment.

The clues to healing human destructiveness are inside each of us, where we clearly wish not to look. Were we to dare, we might rediscover the concept of real rehabilitation. We might develop and sentence first-time offenders to specialized and secure psychiatric inpatient experiences designed to connect them with their feelings and those of others. We might more aggressively ferret out cases of child abuse and mentor victims into adulthood. Solutions would come to us.

Finally, we might abandon the goal of punishment for the goal of healing—them *and* us.

# AFTERWORD

Whoever fights monsters should see to it that in the process he does not become a monster. And when you look long into an abyss, the abyss also looks into you.

—Friedrich Nietzsche

Writing this book has required a willingness to use power coupled with the resolve not to use it maliciously. John Kappler, after all, did not agree to an examination of his psyche; I have attempted to impose one on him. I have been gripped by a mixture of anxiety and excitement in unearthing parts of his life story without his consent, as if exploring the rooms of a darkened home while its owner is away.

When Kappler's daughter Elsie telephoned me one night in tears and begged me to stop writing this book, I felt the same coupling of empathy and resolve that I often feel when burrowing toward the truth with "well-defended" patients. I even took the intensity of her emotions as evidence that my research, of which she was aware, must be bringing me close to core truths about her father.

In addition to the use of force inherent in unauthorized biography, I have wondered whether my writing has been fueled by a measure of anger. My friend, after all, was killed by John Kappler.

I have imagined Kappler seeing my office floor littered with his high school yearbook, letters from his friends and colleagues, his resumé, newspaper clippings about him, a pen with his name printed on it he once gave away, his medical records, the transcript of his trial.

The receipt from my own stay at the Carter Hotel in New York, where Kappler checked in after killing Paul Mendelsohn, is taped to my wall.

I have imagined Kappler's frustration that he is powerless to stop this exploration of his soul. I have found myself worrying that the stress of exposure might drive him to suicide.

Knowing the dark side of unauthorized biography has been essential to writing a balanced one. I was especially careful repeatedly to offer Kappler the chance to meet with me or even to write his own unedited chapters. I repeatedly sought input from his wife and daughters. I tried more than once to talk at length with Robert Jones, the Birmingham, Alabama, pathologist who considers himself Kappler's closest friend from medical school. Each overture was refused.

Without the benefit of Kappler's perspective (other than that offered during psychological assessments filed with the court), I have carefully examined my own perceptions of him for prejudice. Again and again, I have turned back the tide of anger and revulsion at what he did in order to try to understand why he may have done it.

My work, oddly, has revealed connections between John Kappler and myself. I, too, spent my grade school years running from bullies who, having seen me homesick and in tears more than once, felt free to test my strength with their fists. I felt the same kind of anxiety Kappler talks about facing during the backyard fights his father orchestrated. I worried about leaving school late for fear my tormentors would find me walking home alone.

Part of my initial motivation to become a physician was, like Kappler's, to overcome the sense of deficiency those boys had made me feel, to overtake them and hurt them by forcing them to measure their successes against mine. I used to fantasize that they would come to my office deathly ill, for a medicine no one else could dispense, and I would turn them away. I dreamed more than once that I had killed them.

I had more general experience denying my feelings as well. My family and the community in which I was raised did not foster independence or self-expression. I saw my acceptance to college as a kind of rebirth, admission to a place where no one had heard me called a wimp or seen me run away. Like Kappler, I recreated myself. Without being fully aware of what I was doing, I gradually exorcised any hint of femininity or vulnerability from my voice, mannerisms, and behavior. I was successful enough that others began to describe me aloud, much to my satisfaction, as a man's man, someone who wasn't to be toyed with. They didn't know that the qualities in me they perceived as menacing were nothing more than a callus grown over my emotional injuries.

Like Kappler, I considered arming myself by becoming a lawyer, attracted by the chance to pit my intellect and eloquence against that of others, to do battle in a forum where strength had little to do with muscle mass.

Like him, I decided against going to law school. I worried that the adversarial process would cause the darker side of me to grow—the side I knew could take real joy in defeating others rather than understanding them. Perhaps I also sensed that it would offer me little hope of understanding myself.

A year into medical school, I, like Kappler, considered working as a summer intern at the CIA.

I chose to practice psychiatry because, to my surprise, I found that I resonated strongly with the vulnerable, frightened parts of the psychiatric patients I saw during my medical school rotations. I felt empathically connected to them, and they seemed to respond to me. I now understand that they spoke to parts of myself I had tried to abandon.

By working extensively and in depth with patients and entering psychotherapy myself, I began to recognize the disparities between the persona I had refined and the person I was. I was able to start to let some of my rage go by acknowledging it and sharing it.

Jack Kehoe, Kappler's medical school friend who became a psychiatrist, felt Kappler had little respect for the specialty, seeing it as a field for bleeding hearts. "John was from the school of hard knocks," he said. "You pull yourself up by your bootstraps."

What made for the difference between John Kappler and me? What allowed me eventually to bear knowing and letting others know my pain?

I can't be sure of every reason. I know, however, that I was not born into poverty as he was. I know that I did not have to cope with being physically small. I know that my father, rather than pitting me against my boyhood adversaries, confessed that he had run away from his own. I know that when an egg was broken over my head one Halloween night, he watched my mother wash my hair, and we all laughed together when she joked about people paying good money for egg shampoos. Neither of them was alcoholic. They didn't beat me, one another, or my sister.

I didn't lose anyone I loved when I was a boy. When we were teenagers, my friend and next-door neighbor David Feiven was diagnosed with cancer, but he battled it heroically and survived. I didn't have to feel—or defend against feeling—the full weight of helplessness that John Kappler must have shouldered when his younger brother, Robert, died.

I also know that some of what John Kappler suffered has never been revealed, and probably never will be. It is even possible that he buried the worst of it so deeply that it is lost now even to him.

As I was writing the last pages of this book, in fact, it became clear to me how much of himself John Kappler had managed to keep under wraps. He had put forward a plea in court that made his state of mind on April 14, 1990, the sole issue. His character and, thereby, many of his life experiences were officially irrelevant. He hadn't spoken a word at his trial. He had turned me down again and again for interviews. He or his wife had demanded, sometimes with success and sometimes without, that friends and relatives tell me nothing.

I decided to place one more call to Tommie Kappler to request an interview and was surprised when she returned it minutes later.

She told me at length how angry she was that I had used her husband's name in a *Washington Post* column I had written about him.

"I don't know what your book is about," she said, "but if you want to really help people [by writing], you don't need to use names. I don't have much patience with that. . . . You should be ashamed to do something like that." She hinted that if I were to use a pseudonym for her husband, she might be willing to tell me more about him. But then she made it clear that even the shelter of another name wouldn't make her participation likely.

Moments later, she received a call from Elsie, who apparently told her mother she shouldn't be speaking with me at all.

"I'm gonna terminate the conversation," Tommie said.

But she had one more thing to say. "We're in a position to know all the facts," she cautioned me, "so you'd better be very careful because you're in a risky position."

I had heard words of caution from the Kapplers previously. Before his death during 1993, John Kappler's father had cautioned me to be aware of the anger my work was provoking in his son and Tommie. "They wish you didn't exist," he had said.

# ACKNOWLEDGMENTS

*Without Mercy* would not have been written without encouragement and guidance from my agent, Beth Vesel, and my editor at The Free Press, Susan Arellano.

I also thank Betsy Nolan for taking the writer in me by the hand and walking me through the earliest years of my work.

Judge Robert Barton, a man who loves the law and spent time helping me to understand it, has my sincere appreciation.

Finally, I am grateful to the dozens of individuals who, often after considerable soul-searching, shared their thoughts and feelings about John F. Kappler, Jr. with me.